CHOSEN TO SERVE

Yorkshire Publishing
TULSA

ISBN: 978-1-960810-01-4
Chosen to Serve: The story of a drafted infantryman Vietnam-Cambodia 1969-70

Yorkshire Publishing
1425 E 41st Pl
Tulsa, OK 74105
www.YorkshirePublishing.com
918.394.2665

Published in the USA

CHOSEN TO SERVE

The story of a drafted infantryman
Vietnam-Cambodia 1969-70

Sgt. Michael Whalen

FOREWORD

This is the story of my military service in the Republic of South Vietnam. It is dedicated to all the draftees who served so gallantly in the service of their country.

I saw eighteen- and nineteen-year-old boys become men during the trials and tribulations of war. Very few wanted to be there, but they did the job that they were trained to do.

This book is dedicated to all of those who were "Chosen to Serve."

Sergeant: Michael R. Whalen
Bravo Company
2nd of the 22nd Mechanized Infantry
Triple Duce
Third Squad, Third Platoon
25th Infantry Division
1969-1970

CONTENTS

★　　★　　★

CHAPTER 1
Greetings

Dear Sir:

Greetings, your friends, neighbors, and relatives have Chosen You to Serve in the United States armed forces. You are to report for duty on July 20, 1969, at 8:00 a.m. in Pryor, Oklahoma, Mayes County Court House. I remember thinking, ***None of my friends, neighbors, and relatives chose me!***

I grew up on a small dairy farm about seven miles away from our small home town. We raised gardens and crops and hunted and fished. My mother canned a lot of fruits and vegetables every year. We were fairly self-sufficient in that we produced most of our food. We milked cows every day at 5:30 in the morning and 5:30 in the evening. When you have a dairy---there are no days off.

Every time we had a bit of free time my dad would take me fishing or hunting. The squirrels, rabbits, quail, deer, and ducks provided a lot of our meat when they were in season. As I grew up, I roamed the woods and creeks in our area and learned to hunt, fish, and trap by myself.

I went to a small country school for my elementary learning. Basketball was the main sport that I competed in and I loved to play it. There were a lot of Cherokee students at the school and most of them were excellent athletes.

When I was in the sixth through the eighth-grade, I and two other sixth graders started on the eighth-grade basketball team. In the 6th through 8th grade we played 68 basketball games and won all of them.

After I graduated from grade school, I went to my home town high school. I played baseball, football, and basketball. Although I enjoyed playing baseball and football, basketball was still my favorite sport to play.

We had a pretty successful high school basketball career. We never won the state tournament, but in both my junior and senior years during the regular season, we defeated, or came close to defeating, the teams that won the state tournament.

Three of the four seniors on my team received basketball scholarships to junior colleges. One of my best friends and I received scholarships to the same junior college, and the other friend to a different junior college.

The junior college athletic dorm had a large lobby with a TV, and I would go there about every evening to watch the news. We knew about the war in Vietnam, and we all had college deferments from the draft. One evening as I was watching the news the headline was entitled: "The Death of a Marine". They showed a film of Marines quickly moving through a large clearing and shots rang out. One Marine fell to the ground. I remember thinking: That young Marine just lost his life, I hope that they end this war quickly!

The thought went through my mind that someday I may have to be there if it doesn't end soon. When I graduated from junior college I went to Northeastern State University in Tahlequah, Oklahoma to finish my degree.

I worked in the summers at various jobs and on the weekends during school I worked at a gas station to make money to help get me through college.

In December 1966, I married my high school sweetheart. On September 9, 1968, we had our first child. She was a sweet baby girl that we named Kimberly.

In 1968 when I graduated from N.S.U. I got a job teaching and coaching at my hometown school. I was the junior high boys and girls' head coach and the high school boy's assistant coach. I helped coach 17 and 18-year-old kids in high school football. Little did I know that I would be leading kids of that age in combat just a year later.

At the end of my first school year to coach and teach I received my draft letter.

I kissed my wife and baby girl goodbye and left for adventures unknown.

★　★　★

CHAPTER 2
Basic Training

U pon receiving my draft letter, I reported at the time and place shown on the notice. Five draftees and one that volunteered for the draft were issued tickets for Oklahoma City. The one that volunteered for the draft was my brother-in-law, who had just graduated from high school and had gotten married to my wife's youngest sister. He said that he knew that we were going to be drafted so he volunteered to go at the same time as me. We were hoping that we could stay together, but he was assigned to a different company than me. I only saw him once during basic training and none during advanced infantry training.

We were sent to Oklahoma City because it was the nearest military induction center for us. At the induction center, we were given a physical. It was a thorough medical physical. It also included a vision test. I passed it fine. A Native American who I knew that lived in a neighboring town that went by the nick name, "Beans" was drafted at the same time and was also taking the physical and eye test. The test consisted of putting a paddle over one eye and reading the letter on whichever line the administrator told you to read. He told Beans to put the paddle over his right eye and read line five, which was the line with the smallest letters. Beans said, "Can't see it," then he said, read line two, Beans said, "Can't see it." Then the administrator told him to read line one. Line one was the letter "N," and it was about five inches tall. Beans answered, "Can't see it." The guy that was giving the test said, "You go stand in the corner and we will deal with you later." I don't know what happened to Beans, but we never saw him again.

When they gave us the blood pressure test mine was high. They told me that I would be given a room in a nearby hotel and that I was to report back at 8:00 a.m. the next morning.

The next day I went through the physical again and this time they said that my blood pressure was normal. Then they marched about 25 of the ones that passed to physical into the next room, where we were told that we would be inducted into the United States Armed Forces. They told us to raise our right hand and repeat the oath after them. After the conclusion of the oath, the administrator told us to take one step forward and we will officially be in the United States Armed Forces. No one stepped forward and there was a moment of silence, then the instructor giving the oath said, "That's all right; you are in the Armed Forces anyway".

Then we marched into another large room where there were about thirty guys and we were instructed to get in a line. Then we were informed that every other man in line would be a Marine or an Army Soldier. I leaned out and tried to count from the front of the line and they were Army, Marine, Army, Marine. When I got to the man in front of me it was Army and that left me a Marine. So I was mulling over where I would be sent for training as a Marine, but when they got to me they said U.S. Army. I had counted wrong! They told all the men who were to be Marines to report downstairs to board buses that were waiting to take them to Camp Pendleton, California. They lined up the Army draftees and told us that we would be boarding buses for Tiger Land Infantry Training at Fort Polk, Louisiana.

We arrived at Fort Polk at about 2:30 a.m. I remember getting off the bus and smelling the pine trees. Some Private E-1 lined us up in formation and told us, "Anyone who has any kind of a knife or sharp instrument to take them out of their pocket and lay them on the ground." He went around and picked up all the pocketknives that were laid down. Then he started messing with us. He would say, "You guys want to smoke?" All the smokers would say, "Yes sir." I didn't smoke, so it didn't affect me, but he played with the guys that lit up. Right after they lit their cigarettes he yelled, "Put them out." Everyone put out their cigarette and every 4 or 5 minutes he would do it again. This went on for about 30 minutes and every time he would assure them that this time they could smoke. Later we would find out that a Private E-1 had no power over us. We got a laugh out of it later.

We were taken into an infirmary where they lined us up and gave us shots in each arm with air guns. We were told not to flinch because the air guns could cut if we moved. Three guys in line fainted when it came time to get the shots.

We then marched to a supply building where we were issued boots, fatigues, hats, socks, shorts, and t-shirts. Size didn't seem to matter. Some troops' uniforms were too big, and some almost too little. After getting our uniforms they marched us to our company area. It was about 3:45 in the morning and our drill sergeant taught us how to arrange our stuff in our footlocker and how to make our bunk where a quarter would bounce on it when dropped. Then we were told to rack out, so we all went to bed. About 5 minutes later a Lieutenant and the Senior Drill Sergeant came busting through the door banging on metal trash cans with batons and yelling, "FALL OUT, FALL OUT." Once outside they formed us into a formation and had us do about 3 or 4 sets of push-ups. We were then allowed to return to our bunk to sleep. This charade was repeated time after time until about 4:30 in the morning. It was then they finally let us get some sleep.

Every morning we were woken up at 4:30 a.m. by the banging on a trash can with a baton. We had 5 minutes to get dressed and make our bunk. Then we fell out in our company area and were put in formation and marched to breakfast chow. We were not allowed to talk when we were at any chow time. If you talked, you didn't get to eat and had to go outside and do pushups while everyone else ate.

We went to classes all day long. The first class was learning to march and stay in step. We were issued M14 rifles to train with and had a class in order arms, present arms, and right shoulder arms. Then we had an hour of physical training. After the P.T. we were marched to the chow hall for lunch. The next class was more training on marching, left face, right face, eyes right, road guards post, forward march, and rear march. This went on for about 2 hours. Then we had a weapons class on disassembling and assembling our M14 rifles. Also, the cleaning of the weapon. Then more marching training. We started learning the march songs that were used to help get us in shape while we were marching or double timing. The drill sergeant would sing the first line and we were to repeat it as we marched, songs such as: Around her neck she wore a yellow ribbon, she wore a yellow ribbon in the merry month of May, she wore a yellow ribbon for her trainee who was far, far away, she wore a yellow ribbon for her trainee who was far, far away. Another was: I want to be an airborne ranger, I want to live a life of danger, I want to go to Vietnam, I want to kill some Charlie Cong – can't wait, all the way – airborne – ranger, Rahh, Rahh. Sometimes we would sing, "I don't want to go to Vietnam, I don't want to kill no Charlie Cong." We were dropped for many, many pushups for saying that. Nearly everywhere we went to a class we were double-timed, which means running. After this, we marched back to the P.T. field for another hour of physical training. Then we marched back to the company area and were told to take a shower and get ready to go for evening chow. We had about an hour to write letters and rest a little. We were called for reveille and marched to chow. We returned to our barracks and were told to check the list on the bulletin board for fire guard duty. Our barracks were two-story buildings, and they were only about 15 yards apart. I was the first one on the list for the fire guard on the upstairs floor. It was close to lights out when four Black guys in our unit started shouting at some other Black trainees in the window of the barracks next to ours. I don't know what the problem was, but it escalated into both saying they were going to cut up the other one. Finally, they both yelled, "I'll meet you outside and cut you bad." We were not supposed to have knives, but I could see that they both had switchblade knives. I thought I better go get Drill Sergeant Winchester.

The company headquarters was just across the street from our barracks. I ran across the street and went into the office and Drill Sergeant Winchester had his feet up on his desk and his smokey bear hat pulled down over his eyes. I said, "Drill sergeant, there are some guys with knives and they are saying that they are going to cut each other." Without looking up he said, "Blacks"? I said, "Yes, drill sergeant." They are out in front of the barracks ready to stab each other. He slowly took his feet down, pushed his hat back, and slowly walked out to the street. The guys were shouting threats at each other and each one's friends were holding them back. We walked up to them and when they saw Drill Sergeant Winchester they became quiet. He looked at the guy from my platoon and asked him, "Do you want to cut him"? He yelled, "Yea, I'm going to cut his liver out." Then he turned to the other one and asked him the same question and the guy acted like he was trying to get loose from his friends who were holding him back, and he yelled that he was going to cut his heart out. Drill Sergeant Winchester said, "You want to cut him?" and turned to the other one and said, "You want to cut him?" Both said yes. After a slight pause, Drill Sergeant Winchester sternly said to the ones holding both back – "Let Them Go!" They slowly let go and nothing happened. Slowly, they both started backing up and headed back to the barracks. Sergeant Winchester told them to drop the knives and go to bed. He gathered up the knives he walked by me on his way back to the headquarters. He said, "Seen it before!"

Our Senior Drill Sergeant's name was Wally Wahlema; he was a Lima Indian from Arizona, I think. He was a good drill instructor and he looked like Smokey the Bear with his big barrel chest and smokey bear hat pulled down by his eyes. I think he cared for us receiving the proper training for where we were going to go. When we graduated from Basic Training, he gave a short speech and wished us luck you could see tears in his eyes because he knew that some of us would not be coming home from Vietnam alive.

The basic training consisted of several subjects and activities. We did a lot of double-time running and 2 hours a day of exercise. We had classes on disassembling and assembling weapons. They consisted of an M14 rifle, M16 rifle, M60 machine gun, and 45 caliber semiautomatic pistol. We had classes on hand-to-hand combat and bayonet use. They had football helmets that we put on to practice bayonet training, and a big stick with pads on both ends that we plummeted each other with to practice sparring and stabbing methods. We practiced low crawling in the low crawl pits. We climbed over and through obstacle courses, and we went to firing ranges for live fire for the M14, M16, M60, and 45-caliber pistols. We ran the mile every day with t-shirts, pants, and combat boots on.

The drill sergeant kept telling us that at the end of basic training, there would be a test and that the Battalion Commander said that of the 4 training companies in the Battalion, the one that scored the highest on the test would get a three-day pass and win a trophy for him. So, all our training was supposed to be focused on us winning the trophy. Every one of us wanted to win it so that we could get the three-day pass.

Some of the events to be tested were the mile run in combat boots, the 100-yard man carry, the low crawl pit crawl, disassembling and assembling weapons in a certain amount of time, crawling under barbwire for 20 meters, the softball throw, and the obstacle course – all timed events.

You had a certain amount of time to finish each event to max the test. The goal was for every man in our company to max the test.

We were fed three meals a day and each was at the same time every day. Those trainees that were overweight lost weight and those underweight gained weight.

In basic training, there were trainees from all parts of the country with many different speech patterns. People from the eastern states talked very fast and some from the south with a Southern drawl and slower country speech from the southwest. People would say to you, "Say something I want to hear you talk." We thought that it was funny that guys from different areas wanted to hear other guys talk. After about three months of training, all the speech patterns changed. The fast talkers slowed down and the slower talkers sped up. It was sort of a melting pot.

At the end of four weeks of training, they told us that we would get the coming Sunday off, that we could go into town or go home for the few that lived close, and that family could visit us. They marched us to a group of telephone booths and let us call home. Everyone was limited to 5 minutes. I called my wife and told her that they were giving us the coming Sunday off and that if she could try to come, we would have one day together. I received a letter from her on Thursday of the week and she wrote that she and my sister and brother-in-law were coming to see me. They were driving a yellow Volkswagen Bug. It was wonderful to be with my wife and family members even for a day. They had to head home about 5:00 p.m. that day and I kissed my wife goodbye, and they were on their way home. I remember wishing that I could go home with them.

It was back to the grind the next morning we went to the firing ranges for 3 or 4 days and fired live rounds. We were graded on our shooting abilities to see if we qualified for each weapon. We fired M16, M14, and M60 machine guns and 45 caliber pistol rounds. I qualified as an expert in all four weapons.

One day we double-timed to the anti-tank firing range and had training on the M72 LAW antitank weapon. The weapon is a shoulder-fired rocket that could penetrate several inches of steel. We each got to fire one rocket down range at old tanks so that we could get the feel of the weapon. It was kind of fun to fire them.

We went to First-Aid classes where we were instructed on how to bandage different types of wounds. We were instructed on how and when to give someone morphine. They gave each of us a dummy morphine tube with a needle on the end, and we got to practice how to administer it to some dummy soldiers. We learned how to bandage a sucking chest wound. Most of us had never heard of a sucking chest wound, but we soon learned that if the wound wasn't sealed off soon that person could die from collapsed lungs.

We also had a class on poisonous snakes. We learned how to identify them and how to try to avoid getting bitten. There were lots of snakes on Fort Polk. The poisonous snakes consisted of copperheads, pygmy rattlesnakes, cottonmouths, and coral snakes. We were told that the coral snake was the deadliest because of their nerve toxin venom, but that they had set fangs and that they could only bite places such as between your fingers or on the edge of your ear.

We were instructed on the number and kinds of poisonous snakes in Asia. There were so many kinds you couldn't remember them all. The most impressive ones were the black and green mambas and the cobras. The green mambas were called two steppers in Vietnam because it was said that after you were bitten you got two steps before you died.

One day after we were marched to our barracks, we were released to our bunks and given one and a half hours to read and write letters, shower, and get ready to sack out. I was good friends with three guys from Iowa—Mark and Mack Wald who were twins, and Dwayne Tietjen. They were all from around the Dubuque area in Iowa. All of them were farm boys. The twins and I were reading and writing letters and after a while Mark said, "Where is Dwayne?" I said "I don't know" I didn't see him leave. We were not supposed to leave the company area, so we started looking for him. We couldn't find him, so we went back upstairs to our bunking area. Shortly after that we heard someone come running up the stairs and someone was after him. It was Dewayne and he was drunk. He had slipped out to the P.X. and downed three 24 oz cups of beer. He started chasing some black guys around their bunks and yelling that he was going to beat the hell out of them. I told Mark he was going to get in trouble if we don't do something. We both started talking to him saying, "Dewayne you don't want to fight those guys, they haven't done anything to you." He said, "Yea I do, get out of my way." While we were trying to get him to stop the black guys made it down the stairs. When he turned and saw that they were gone he said, "I'll just whip all of your butts." Mark and I kept talking to him and telling him you don't want to fight us we are your friends. He said, "Yea, I do" and started toward us. Mark whispered to me and said we're going to have to knock him out for his good. Dewayne was a 6 foot 3 inch muscled up rawboned Iowa farm boy. He would be hard to handle. Mark said, "You get behind and grab him and I will hit him." I said, "You get behind him and grab him and I'll hit him." He quickly replied, "Ok, but hit him good." I kept talking to Dewayne while Mark worked his way behind him. When he wasn't looking Mark grabbed him from the back and Dewayne started spinning around Mark yelled, "Hit him, hit him!" I stepped up and hit him in the chin when he came around and he stopped spinning. We thought it got him, but all of a sudden,

22

he went berserk and started spinning Mark around again. Mark was yelling, "Hit him again, hit him again. I can't hold him much longer." The next time he came around I hit him as hard as I could on the back of his jaw, and he went limp.

We carried him over to his bunk, which was right next to mine, and put him in it. I told the twins if he comes to we were going to be in trouble again. Mack suggested that we take a bed sheet and rip it into strips to tie him to his bunk. It didn't take us long to get that accomplished. We tied each arm and leg to a different corner of the bed. Shortly after we had finished tying him up it was time for lights out, and we all went to sleep.

When they turned on the lights and banged on the metal trash cans to wake us up the next morning, I sat up on my bunk and looked at Teage as we called him. I wondered what kind of trouble we would have from him this morning. I looked across the aisle and looked at Mack and he nodded that he was ready. We didn't know what to expect. Dewayne woke up and he slowly looked at each leg and each wrist and then at me. Then he said, "Untie me". I thought well, we might as well get it over with. After I had untied him, he slowly sat up on his bunk and said to me, "What happened?" I told him that you came in drunk last night and you were trying to fight everybody that you came across including Mark, Mack, and me, so we knocked you out and tied you to your bunk so that you wouldn't get in trouble. He sat there for a while without saying anything and then slowly raised his head and said, "If I do it again just knock me out and tie me up again."

Dewayne was one of the nicest guys you could ever meet – if he was sober – but boy we found out he could be one of the meanest you ever met when he was drunk. He never did sneak out and do that again.

Our basic training continued much the same. We did two hours of physical training each day and had more weapons training.

We were on bivouac training out in the field where we slept in pup tents. One day when we were marching to a mess tent that had been set up to feed us lunch we noticed a sharp curve in the dirt road just before we got to the mess tent. Drill Sergeant Walima had us ground our steel pot liners and weapons right past the curve and then marched us to the tent to get ready to eat. We heard a duce and half-food track coming, fast around the curve in the road and he ran over some helmets, and weapons before he saw them. Some of us kind of chuckled and the drill sergeant and lieutenant said, "You think that's funny, give me 25 pushups!" After 25 pushups and after we finished, I guess I was the only one still smiling. The lieutenant came up to me and chewed me out and dropped us all to the front leaning rest, which is the up-pushup position. He told me to take my left hand and wipe the smile off my face and then spit on it. It was all I could do to get rid of the smile, but I finally did.

About the second week in October, they finally gave us a three-day pass. I booked a flight to get home and back so that I would have a little more time at home with my wife and baby girl.

Two of my friends from Louisiana, Tom Tanney Hill and Tom Broom, both begged me to go home with them and that they would take me deer hunting. They said we use dogs and swamp buggies to hunt deer in the swamps and it is a lot of fun. I told them that I would like to do that sometime, but that I had to go home to see my family.

My wife, her uncle, aunt, and my daughter picked me up at the Tulsa, Oklahoma airport. It was good to be home even if it was just a short while. I was able to be at home for almost two days before having to fly back.

After arriving back at Fort Polk it was back to the grind. We had fire and maneuver training with blank rounds for our rifles. Then we had hand grenade training with dud grenades. We had to go through a tough obstacle course every day for the last few weeks.

Then there was the gas chamber. They had a tent set up and it was filled with C.S. gas. And just before you went in you had to put your gas mask on. When it was your turn you went in and you had to hold your weapon between your knees and put your helmet on the barrel, then remove your gas mask and say your name, rank and serial number, and the serial number of your weapon. They did this so that you would have to take in some of the gas. Then the sergeant would say go and you would run out the back door. It didn't take you very long to figure out which way the wind was coming from and you would face right into it because of the burning eyes, nose, and mouth. It usually took about five minutes before you sort of got over the burn and watery eyes, nose, and mouth.

It finally came time for us to take the test that we were being told about the whole time that we were in basic training. Some of the things that were on the test were 100-meter man carry on your back, softball throw, run the mile in combat boots, 50-meter crawl in the low crawl pits under a certain amount of time, how many monkey bars that you could get in one minute, how long it took you to go through the obstacle course, disassembling and reassembling all weapons in a certain amount of time. All the events that were on the test had to be achieved in a certain amount of time to max them. Most of us in the training company that I was in maxed all the events.

Tom Tanneyhill, who was a high school state track star, set the record at Fort Polk for running the mile in combat boots.

When all the test results were in from all of the training companies they put us in formation and announced that we had won the Colonel Trophy. A big cheer went up because they had told us that if we won the trophy we would get a three-day pass.

The next day was graduation day and they passed out khaki dress uniforms for us to wear while we marched in front of the grandstands in the parade. They had told us that we would get our three-day pass after graduation, so we had all made plans to go home for three days. We were marching back to the company area and held in formation. They handed us our new orders and promotions. I was to report to North Fort Polk for Tigerland advanced infantry training and was promoted to Private E-2 which came with a five-dollar-a-month raise. I kept five dollars a month and sent the rest home to my wife who could barely get by on ninety dollars a month. It was quite a cut in pay from the five hundred a month that I was getting for teaching and coaching back home.

While we were in formation someone asked the drill sergeant, when will we get our three-day pass? He said you will get it when you get to your next duty station. Senior Drill Sergeant Wally Walima, who was well-liked by us, wished us good luck and told us that he hoped that what we had learned would help us to survive. Tears came to his eyes when he said that because he knew where most of us were going and that some wouldn't be coming back alive.

Buses arrived at our company area, and we were released to get on the buses. We were told that they were taking us to our new company area at North Fort Polk Tigerland Advanced Infantry Training.

CHAPTER 3
AIT Tigerland

The buses dropped us off at our new company area at North Fort Polk. We were now in Tigerland advanced infantry training. They told us that the training would be some of the toughest training that the U.S. Army had to offer.

There were 160 men in our training company. They put us in formation with our dress uniforms on. Someone whispered, "Now they are going to release us for our three-day pass."

After a short speech, the Company Commander released us to our platoon drill sergeant, and we were taken to our barracks and assigned a bunk and locker. We stashed our duffle bags in the trunk lockers then the drill sergeants told us to change into fatigues. Then we were told to fall out for another company formation. I heard someone whisper again, "Now they are going to release us for the pass that we were promised."

They marched us to a large field behind the company area and had us spread out in line. Then we were instructed to start pulling grass. For our three-day pass, we got to be human lawnmowers for the next three days. Needless to say, no three-day pass!

Our Tigerland training started with more weapons training and a lot more running and exercises. We went to a firing range to shoot our M16s and sight them in. We spent almost a whole day firing the M16s on semi-automatic and some on fully automatic weapons in 3 to 5-round burst to keep the barrel from getting too hot and having rounds cook off before they were fully chambered.

One day we went to the M79 grenade launcher range we were instructed on how to fire them and what the kill zones were for the different types of rounds. There were impact explosive rounds, flechette rounds, and what were called bouncing Betty rounds. The kill range for the impact explosive rounds was 5 meters and the kill zone for the bouncing Betties was 15 meters and the flechette rounds were like a big shotgun. We were also trained to tilt them up and fire like a mortar if the situation called for it.

We had to learn our service number and the serial number of the M16 that was issued to us, and anytime that we were asked we had to repeat them along with the statement: This is a M16 A-1 5.56 caliber semi-auto-fully auto weapon; there are many like it, but this one is mine.

We spent another day at the M16 firing range that had pop-up targets. One skinny kid that the drill sergeants had been harassing because he couldn't shoot well totally lost it, and he turned and sprayed the viewing tower with several rounds of live ammunition. The soldier next to him tackled him and the drill instructors restrained him. I could tell by looking at his face that the pressure that had been put on him by the drill sergeants had made him crack. Luckily, no one was hit by his bullets. The MPs came and took him away, and we never saw him again. One day we marched to the M72 Law Anti-tank weapon firing range. They had rows of old tanks and other tracked vehicles scattered down range at different distances. We were instructed on how to arm and aim and fire the weapons. In the afternoon we were allowed to fire 2 rockets each so that we could get the feel of the weapon. I remember the first one that I fired I was expecting some kind of recoil when I pushed the firing button, but nothing happened, so I thought that it didn't fire. So I pushed the fire button again. Just as I pushed the button the second time the round hit the tank that I was aiming at and exploded. Amazing no recoil!

That afternoon we were double-timed to a 45-caliber pistol firing range. They had man-shaped form targets that we fired at. I had never shot a semi-automatic pistol before. The only big caliber pistols that I had ever shot were revolvers that kicked up and I was expecting the same with the 1911 45 caliber pistol. I aimed the first round at the bottom of the target – and guess what? – that is exactly where the round hit. I quickly realized that the semiauto pistol hit where you aimed.

Next on our advanced training agenda was more training with the 50 cal. They put on demonstrations of the effectiveness of the 50 cal. It could shoot through four times thick cement blocks and shoot through trees that were two feet thick.

We all got to fire three one-hundred-round belts of ammo. We were taught how to clean and clear the weapon and how to change a barrel when it was getting too hot. Also, they told us that the enemy's answer to the 50 calibers was a 51 caliber machine gun, and our rounds would fire in their 51 calibers, but their 51 caliber bullets wouldn't fire in our 50 calibers. Also, we learned that our big mortars were 81 millimeters and that theirs were 82 millimeters, and the same was true of them as the machine guns. They could fire our 81 MM mortars in their tubes, but we couldn't fire their 82 MMs in our mortar tubes.

We had one guy in our barracks that would not take a shower and all the guys around his bunk started complaining about the odor. They started leaving little hints on his bunk, such as a towel and a bar of soap on his pillow. We would watch him to see what he would do. He would take the stuff and put it in his locker. We didn't know if he was embarrassed to get J-bird naked with 20 or 30 other guys in the showers or what his problem was. Finally, a note was left on his pillow to take a shower or he would be given a soap party. We watched him read the note and go put it in his locker and go to bed. After about 30 minutes the guys that bunked around him slipped out of their bunks and they all wrapped a bar of soap in a towel and twisted it up. Some guys went to the showers and turned the water on fairly hot. He was asleep and they started hitting him all over with the soap towels. He started screaming and crying and I felt sorry for him. Then they grabbed him up and dragged him to the showers. They stripped him of his shorts and shoved him in the shower, and every time he would try to get out they would shove him back in. Two guys in the shower with him had bathroom stool scrub brushes and they were brushing him with them. He was crying and sobbing and I felt sorry for him again. I told the guys that were doing it "That's enough," and they finally stopped harassing him. Not a word was said about the incident. The next night he went to the shower and took a shower. It was harsh treatment, but it worked. He took showers from then on.

We went on about a four-mile march into the woods and we came upon about a five-acre clearing. They had a big communications tent set up and bleachers for the class that they were going to present to us on navigation skills. We were taught how to use a compass and we had to learn how many of our walking steps and our running steps equaled 10 meters. After we had some practice, they told us that we would have to go on a nighttime compass course that night. We were given some short objectives to practice in the daytime. They let us pick a partner and Dewayne Tietjen and I teamed up. As we were doing the short daytime course in the woods, we saw several copperheads, pygmy rattlers, and coral snakes! We thought this was going to be bad at night.

Right before dark, we were given a compass and a list of eight objectives that we were to navigate to. They also gave us a small flashlight and a pencil and a pad. When we reached an objective, we were to write down what was on the sign that was nailed to a tree, and also it would give the next coordinates and the distance to it.

We were about the third team to be released on the course right at dark. They were setting teams off in 15-minute intervals. Tietjen and I had agreed that I would run the compass and that he would do the counting. I aimed the compass at a distant object and told Tietjen to start counting. We had to keep the flashlight off so that we could see the silhouette of our aiming point, which was usually a predominant tree on the horizon. Every time that we turned the flashlight on we would see a snake. So we talked it over and we decided to run instead of walking because we thought we might have less of a chance of being bitten.

The first objective was 300 meters on a 60-degree compass reading. I was running behind Tietjen and all at once he came to an abrupt stop. He said, "We're here!" I turned the flashlight on and sure enough on a tree directly ahead of us was a white sign. I remember the saying on the first sign was 'Blue Bird Hill.'

We wrote that on our cards and wrote down the next coordinates and distance. I picked up an object and pointed it out and Tietjen took off running again with me after him. Each time on all eight objectives when he stopped, I would turn on the light and in the nearby area I would find the sign. We would write down the sayings and coordinates at each one and head for the next.

The last coordinates would take us back to the big communications tent where all the drill sergeants and officers were settling in chairs.

When we broke into the clearing, we stopped running and walked up to the tent, and went inside. One of the drill sergeants who was leaning back in a chair said, "What's the deal, did you all get lost?" We said, "No we're through." Two or three of the sergeants said, "No way, this is a 3- to 4-hour compass course. I said, "We ran all the way and there is our card with what we were supposed to write down at each objective." They all looked at our cards, and finally, the captain said, "The fastest anyone has ever finished this course is 1 hour and 15 minutes and you two did it in 31 minutes. That is a new record." I don't know if we still hold the record or not, but with all the running we didn't get snake bit!

One thing I noticed about the Army instructors was that they were very good teachers. After you finish your training with them, you would not forget it.

Our next training was on armored personnel carriers. We learned that their purpose was to get troops safely to the fight as quickly as possible in a protected enclosure. We also learned that it was not feasible because if you were inside the track and it hit a mine, the concussion would kill everyone inside. So, we were told that everyone in Vietnam rode on top of the tracks, not in them.

For part of our APC training, we did get sealed up inside and crossed a pond underwater to show us that APCs could cross water that was deeper than the track was tall.

Our next training was more hand-to-hand combat and bayonet training. We were taught several ways to kill people with our bare hands. We practiced the moves on each other, of course without following through with the kill.

In bayonet training, they had big sticks with a pad on each end that you would use to parry off the other guys' padded sticks. They put us in two lines facing each other about 20 meters apart. We put on football helmets for protection. Then when they blew the whistle, you would rush each other and try to knock the other guy down with your padded stick. It was pretty brutal training. We learned how to fix bayonets, and then we went to a course where you ran through and stabbed all the targets as you came to them.

The day after the bayonet training, I woke up with a toothache. They let me go to the dentist on the base. Two young dentists checked me and told me that I had four bad jaw teeth and that they were going to pull all four of them. I asked them, "Can't you fix them?" One of them said, "No, we are going to pull them because where you are going you are not going to need them anyway." He didn't know how close I was to punching his arrogant lights out. I needed help, so they pulled all four teeth. With four teeth pulled, I was given the rest of the day off.

The next training that we went through was BB gun training. The instructor told us that in the Nom, you may never have time to aim your weapon in a firefight. He said that most of the fighting was at fairly close range, and about ninety percent of the firefights would be at night. We were told that we would spend five days training with the BB guns. The BB guns were all Daisy pump guns.

The instructor flipped an aspirin into the air and quickly pointed his BB gun at it and busted it in the air. Then he did it again, and everyone was very impressed that he could do that. Then he told us that every one of us would be able to bust an aspirin in the air at the end of the training.

On the first day, they divided us up into teams of two. We were issued a big packet of BBs, a Daisy pump, a clear plexiglass face shield, and a stack of medallions that were each the size of a silver dollar. We spent all day taking turns throwing up the medallions while the other tried to hit the metal disk with BBs, and at the end of the first day, we could point and shoot and hit the big disk almost every time.

The second day was the same except the disk that they gave us to use that day was the size of a half-dollar, at the end of that day we were getting pretty good at the point-and-shoot thing.

On the third day, the disk dropped to the size of a quarter. This training was fun and we gained a lot of confidence in our ability to point and shoot and hit.

On the fourth day, the medallion was the size of a nickel, and at the end of the day, we were consistently hitting them in the air. On the last day, the medallion was the size of a dime. This was working and we were getting very good at this point-and-shoot game.

The next morning, we were marched to some bleachers with a stage and the instructor said that each one of us would come to the stage and bust an aspirin to qualify for the training. It took almost all morning, but nearly every one of the 120 men busted an aspirin on stage.

Then we were told that we would go through a sniper-detecting trail through the thick woods in the afternoon. There would be seven snipers hidden somewhere along the trail. They said to take our time and check trees and bushes, and if you see them before they see you, you could shoot them above the waist with your Daisy pump. If they saw you before you saw them, they could shoot you anywhere above the belt. Everyone had a clear safety shield to wear to protect their eyes.

The trail was very much like a jungle because of all the vines, trees, and bushes. They released one man at a time 10 minutes apart, and they said to take your time and be very alert. As I was sneaking down the trail I could hear shouts of "OH" and some curse words as different people were being shot with the BB guns. I took my time and I saw six out of the seven snipers before they saw me and I shot them in the chest with my BB gun, but the seventh one saw me first. He was up high in a tree and hiding behind the trunk. He shot me right in the center of my belt buckle and I waved thanks to him because he shot me where it didn't hurt.

The BB gun training was probably the most important training that we received. In Vietnam, we learned what they told us was very true, that about 90% of the time you didn't have time to aim your weapon and you developed an instinctive reaction to point and shoot to try to stay alive. We were trained to build up fire superiority in a firefight and the faster you could do that the better chance you had of winning.

After finishing the BB gun training, we marched back to the company area and while we were in formation the Company Commander announced that we were getting a three-day pass. We would be getting off Friday, Saturday, and Sunday, and had to be back for reveille on Monday morning. A big yell went up from the troops as we were very happy and surprised because we were not expecting the pass.

All the troops who would have time to catch a bus or plane home and back made plans to go home. The ones who lived too far away for it to be feasible went into Lees Ville for their pass just to get away from the fort for a while. I tried to set up air travel home and back, but I couldn't make connections of flights going home, but I did set up a schedule for flying back. I called the Greyhound bus station and set up connections to get home. I could get home 6 hours faster on the bus than I could on a flight with the 5-hour layover in Dallas.

The Greyhound buses came to our company area on Thursday evening and we were released to board them. The only stop we would have where we got off the buses was in Baton Rouge. We had a 30-minute stop. Tom Broom and Tom Tanneyhill, who were friends of mine, exited there because they both lived close to there out in the country. They invited me to go down the street with them to see the sights. I had never seen so many bars and eating joints. It was like being in a movie or something. We got a hamburger and a beer, and then I looked at my watch to see what time it was. I had 10 minutes before my bus was to leave. I quickly told Broom and Tanneyhill that I had to go. I'd have to run to make it. I ran back to the bus stop and caught the bus just as it was getting ready to pull out.

I arrived in Pryor, Oklahoma at about daylight after riding the Greyhound bus all night. I called my wife from a payphone, and she and our daughter came to pick me up. I was very glad to see both of them and glad to be home – even if it was for a short while.

We went out to visit my parents that afternoon. Deer season was open and my dad told me that he had built a tree stand for me in a big pecan tree in a large meadow. The next morning, I was in the tree with my rifle before daylight. About twenty minutes after dawn I saw an eight-point buck and a doe enter the field to the west. They were about one hundred yards away and looked like they were about to get closer, so I took a rest on a limb and squeezed off a shot. The buck fell and the doe ran off. I got a buck on my three-day pass.

The three-day break passed too quickly and before you knew it, it was time to go to the airport and fly back to North Fort Polk. My wife and baby and her uncle and aunt took me to Tulsa to the airport. I kissed my wife and baby girl goodbye and boarded the plane back to the fort.

After arriving back at Tigerland the next day, it was back to training grind. We had another day of first aid training where we learned how to give morphine for pain, put bandages on different types of wounds, and how to put direct pressure on wounds to help stop the bleeding. We spent the rest of the day practicing putting bandages on each other and mannequins, and also more CPR training. We practiced CPR training on dummies made for training.

The next training that we received was how to communicate on the PRICK25 radio. We learned how to start and stop each transmission with our call sign and the call sign of the party that we were contacting. We had to learn the military alphabet as these words were to be used on any radio transmission. A, B, C, D, and E were Alfa, Bravo, Charlie, Delta, and Echo through the alphabet to W, X, Y, and Z which was, Whiskey, X-ray, Yankee, and Zulu. We also learned how to squelch the radio if the enemy was too close for you to answer with talk.

We spent another day with explosive training. We learned about TNT and C-4 plastic explosives. We were instructed on how to use detonating chord (det-chord is clear plastic tubing with C-4 explosives inside) and how to use blasting caps with the det-cord and fuses that were lit with a match or lighter. We also were trained how to use Bangalore torpedoes, which were 7-foot-long metal tubes that were filled with TNT explosives. The Bangalore were threaded on both ends and you could screw them together for a long line of explosives. We were told that this was the best way to blow up and collapse tunnels.

The C-4 plastic explosives took a shock and a spark to set them off. We could light a piece of it and use it to heat our C-rations. You could roll a small ball of C-4 and light it on hard ground and stomp it with your boot and it would go "BANG." We were given some instruction on how to make shape charges so that you could blow up something like a dud bomb and determine which direction the blast would go. The next day, as with every day, we had double time running everywhere we went and two hours of physical training every day no matter what the rest of the training day consisted of.

Mine and booby-trap detection was our next training event on the schedule. The training we were receiving on mine and boob-trap detection in A.I.T was much more in-depth than the training that we received in basic training. We were trained in how to use electronic mine detectors, and how to look for and find hidden trip wires, both on the ground and in the trees. To never pick up or move anything that looked out of the ordinary because it could be booby-trapped. We all got to run the metal detectors and hear what sound they would make when finding a mine. Also, we were trained to use a wooden probe knife if we were probing the ground for a mine or a booby-trap because if they were to be battery detonated, a metal blade could set them off.

We walked through a tripwire course where we walked slowly to see the tripwire before we tripped them either on the ground or in the air. This training turned out to be very helpful. At the end of the training, we were told that several troops in Vietnam were killed when they picked up a zippo cigarette lighter along a trail that they thought another G.I. had dropped, and when they flicked it, it would blow up in their face.

The next training that we had was hand grenade training. The baseball-type grenades weighed four pounds each, and the training on throwing them was more of a shove than a throw. If you extended your arm, you could tear ligaments in your shoulder. We each got to throw three live hand grenades. They had small U-shaped cubicles to throw the grenade from. To qualify, we had to throw the grenade 30 meters either in the air, on the bounce, or on the roll on the ground. A drill sergeant instructor was in the throw pits with each troop one at a time.

One troop who was in the throwing pit next to mine was so scared when he pulled the pin on his first grenade that he dropped it inside the pit and the handle popped off. The sergeant quickly picked it up and dropped it over the front of the cement block pit and yelled for everyone to get down. It exploded and I felt the concussion from it. Luckily no one was hit by the fragments. The man who dropped the grenade got his butt chewed for about five minutes, and I thought, I bet he won't drop the next one.

When we finished the grenade training they marched us back to the company area and while we were in formation they told us that we would be given the coming Sunday off and that we could not leave, but we could have visitors. This was Wednesday so we had three days to notify anyone that lived close enough to come and visit for one day. We were allowed to make one phone call to tell them that they could come and visit. I didn't call because I knew that my wife didn't have the money to buy gas to drive to Fort Polk and back to Oklahoma.

A lot of the guys that were from Louisiana had visitors to come and see them. Some had their family come and some had their girl-friends come. Some of the troops were Cajun and their girlfriends came to visit them. The guys were good-looking dudes, but their girlfriends were some of the most beautiful girls that I had ever seen.

Dewayne Tietjen's parents drove down from Iowa to see him. I guess Tietjen had written to them and told them that I was one of his best friends. After being introduced to them after a while his dad came up to me and asked me, "How is Dewayne doing?" I thought I might as well tell him the truth. I told him what had happened in Basic Training when Dewayne got drunk and mean. He told me that Dewayne was the only child and that they owned a large farm and that they had spoiled him. He said that he knew that Dewayne got mean when he was drinking and that two different times he had almost beaten the men to death. The judge was going to give him two years in jail for the second assault and he said that he negotiated a deal with the Judge that he would volunteer for the draft and that maybe the Army would straighten him up. I told his dad that he hadn't slipped out and drank anymore and that Dewayne was the nicest guy that you could meet when he wasn't drinking.

It was getting close to the end of our AIT training and we were reminded that we would be going on bivouac for seven days and would go through live fire training. Live fire was where three, M60 machine guns on tripods set to fire 36" off of the ground would be firing live rounds over your head in a crossfire while you low crawled 100 yards through the course. Also, there were explosion pits all through the course and they would set off explosives at random while you were crawling under the machine gun fire. The purpose of the live fire training was to see if you would panic or what you would do with the rounds cracking over your head and the explosives lifting you off the ground. They told us it was better to find out now if someone couldn't handle the stress and to not get someone killed in real combat because of their reactions.

It had been fairly hot weather in our training, but a few cold fronts started coming through and cold weather was on its way. The day to go on the seven-day bivouac came. We had prepared our 80-round packs the day before. And were lined up in formation in front of the company area. We could look down the street and see all five other training companies lined up in formation on both sides of our company. It was 18 miles out to the bivouac area and we were told that we would be hauled out there by duce and ½ trucks. We watched the trucks start picking up troops down the street from us and go by. When the next trucks came we thought that it was our turn, but they passed us and picked up the company to our left. We didn't know what to think when the next group of trucks passed us and picked up the last company but us.

After the trucks were out of sight, we were given the command to mount up. That meant putting the 80-pound pack on your back. Then we were given a command of left face and double time "ho". We were trotting with our M16 and 80-pound pack straps cutting into our shoulders. We double-timed about ¼ of a mile downhill and came to an intersection and some whispered maybe the trucks are going to pick us up there at the intersection. Then the order, "Road guards post" came and we ran right on through the intersection.

We were in the 4th platoon which consisted of forty troops. We were on an 18-mile force march, which meant when it was downhill or flat you double-timed, and when uphill you walked. Dewayne Tietjen and I were side by side in the formation and after we had gone about 3 miles people started falling in the ditches because they just couldn't go on carrying the 80-pound pack on their back. Aid vehicles were coming along picking up the guys that were dropping out.

After we had traveled about eight or nine miles the platoons were strung out and the lead platoon was setting the pace. The last platoon in which we were was receiving the whip effect of a long formation. By the time that the lead platoon walked uphill and ran downhill by the time it got back to us, we were running all the time just to keep up. Tietjen and I decided that we would go to the front and set an even pace. The straps biting into our shoulders made them numb.

As we broke formation and started ahead a Lieutenant who was running beside us told us to get back in formation. We got back in formation for a while. More and more guys were dropping out beside the road and in the ditches. We decided to go to the front again and this time as we went by the Lieutenant, he never said anything. He just looked at us because he was having trouble breathing and he didn't even have an 80-pound pack on his back.

When we reached the front we set an even slower pace and finally everyone that was still going caught up and settled into the pace that we were keeping. We had about a mile to go and we could tell that we were in a groove and that we were going to make it.

When we reached our bivouac site only 31 soldiers completed the full pack 18-mile force march. Tietjen and I were the first to get to the finish line. Once we got to the bivouac area we were assigned a position on the perimeter and told to dig and make a fighting position. We had sandbags and our entrenching tools to fill the bags with. We took the rest of the day to build our bunker and line it with sandbags.

The time of the year was early December and the humid heat that we had endured during basic and the first two-thirds of advanced infantry training was over. Cold fronts were coming down from the North and some nights would be freezing. Most of the cold fronts would begin with cold rain and get you wet and when the wind would blow your teeth would chatter. We had goose-down mummy sleeping bags and that was the only thing that saved us from getting hypothermia as we were not allowed to have a fire.

On the second day of "camp out," we were told that we would be doing more fire and movement training and that we would be gassed with CS gas. About thirty minutes before we started the training it came a hard cold rain for about fifteen minutes that got us and almost everything we had soaking wet.

We were to use blank ammunition in our M16s for the training. There was a device that we attached to the end of our gun barrels that created enough back pressure to make the rifles eject the blank cases after they were fired. We were marched to a training area that had pop-up man targets. The area was big enough that we could do our fire and movement operations training there.

As we were doing the training one squad would jump up and run forward for two seconds, then hit the ground while the second squad laid down covering fire, and then the first squad would lay down covering fire while the other moved forward for two seconds. We were told to never stay up for three seconds because that is how long it takes to make a well-aimed shot.

We were about halfway through the area when the drill sergeants and officers started yelling, "Gas, gas, gas!" We immediately put on our gas masks and cleared them as they started popping cans of CS gas right in front of us.

As the clouds of CS gas were drifting up to us, we were to continue our fire and movement operations. As the gas engulfed me I took a breath and my gas mask didn't work. I jumped up and ran out of gas and a drill sergeant started yelling at me to get back. I told him that my gas mask didn't work and I looked around and about twenty more guys were by me choking and coughing, and with burning eyes. They neglected to tell us that if the gas mask filter got wet it would not work. The heavy rain that had soaked us earlier had caused the gas masks to not function.

The next day we had survival training. One part of the training was no chow for us. We were given one whole chicken, an onion, one small packet of salt, and an empty one-gallon can for every two soldiers. We were to cook and eat what we cooked for our three meals that day. My partner and I cut up the chicken, diced up the onion, and put it in the can with salt, pepper, and water. We built a small fire and cooked it for about two hours and that was our survival food for the day. Believe it or not, it wasn't too bad.

Something bad happened to one of the guys in our company that day. We were told to watch out for poisonous snakes, especially the small pygmy rattlesnakes that were abundant in that area. If we had to go to the bathroom we just went out into the woods. He went out in the woods to go to the bathroom and a pygmy rattlesnake bit him on his private parts. He was in pretty bad shape and they flew out in a helicopter to take him to the hospital. We never saw him again so we never knew what happened to him.

Our last day on bivouac was the live fire training that we had been getting ready the whole week for. The night before it turned really cold and sleeted most of the night. It was a miserable night with no fire for heat.

Live fire consisted of three pedestal-mounted M-60 machine guns that traversed back and forth with interlocking fire and explosion pits throughout the course. The live rounds would have tracers on every fifth one and the explosions would be loaded and concussions would be felt. We were told that the machine gun rounds would be 36 inches above the ground and that the explosions in the pits would simulate exploding 82mm mortar rounds.

The live fire course was about a hundred yards long and eighty yards wide. A whole infantry company would go at one time.

The purpose of the training was to see how everyone would react under live fire. If someone was going to crack it would be now not in real combat. All along the far end of the course from the M60s machine guns were a deep ditch and all along the edge were ladders that we were to climb up to the top and low crawl to the other end until you got behind the machine guns.

Our whole company scattered out from one side to the other in the ditch and the guns started firing. You could see the tracers above and hear the rounds cracking. The order was given "over the top" and we climbed the ladders and started low crawling towards the other end. When you crawled close to an explosion pit they would remotely set off an explosive and it would lift you off of the ground. When most of us got about halfway through the course everyone around me started complaining that their elbows and the bottom of their hands were raw and bleeding from all of the low crawling in the wet sand. Mine were the same way. We lay under the fire watching the tracers go over and I said, "The tracers look like the bullets are about 4 feet high instead of 3 feet and I think that we can safely get up on our hands and knees to finish the course. We all did that and finally got behind the guns so that we could stand up.

That completed our bivouac training and we were very glad to see the duce and ½ trucks pull up in front of our company formation and stop. We were going to get to ride back to the company area and not do the 18-mile force march again.

After all the basic and advanced infantry training, I was in the best physical condition of any time of my life. It seemed like we could do the Ranger Run forever without getting tired. I came out of training weighing 200 pounds.

After the bivouac came graduation and another parade. When the parade was over, we marched back to the company area and kept in formation. They called us up to the front one at a time and announced what our orders would be for our next duty station. We were also given our 20-day pass papers. I was promoted to Private 1st Class E-3 and given a $10.00 a month raise. Most of us, myself included, received orders for Vietnam. The National Guard guys received orders for home. Tom Tanneyhill, the Louisiana State Track Champion, who set the record for running the mile in combat boots, got orders to stay at Fort Polk to be on the Fort Polk track team. Dewayne Tietjen got a hardship discharge saying that he was needed on the farm. They gave us or monthly check and released us to a bus that took us to the civilian airport and I flew home on a military discount ticket.

Now there was no question, "I was going to war"! We had all hoped that it would be over by the time our training was complete. I even came real close to signing up for Airborne Ranger training school which was six months more advanced training, thinking that it might be over by then, but I decided to go home for the 20-day pass because I wanted to be with my wife and family as much as I could before I had to go to war.

★ ★ ★

CHAPTER 4

Leaving for War

I enjoyed my 20-day pass at home before I had to leave for Vietnam. I went to visit with family members and hunted and trapped. I trapped to make some extra money for my family. Fur prices were pretty high and I sold them for a pretty good check. My wife and I had been just barely scraping by on private pay, and this money would help her to stay afloat.

The 20 days passed by rapidly and it was time for me to go. I told all my family members goodbye, and I remember my dad told me to take care of myself. My wife took me to catch the plane and we said goodbye to each other and my baby girl. I thought I may never see them again. It was hard to leave.

It was on December 20, 1969, that I left for Fort Lewis in Seattle, Washington. My flight was to land in Denver and then on to Seattle. On airplanes at that time you could sit almost anywhere that you wanted to, so I sat by a window so that I could look out. I remember seeing the snow-covered mountains and thinking how beautiful.

When we landed in Denver about half of the people on the plane disembarked and about 15 minutes later new people started loading on. I was looking out the window when someone touched me on the shoulder and asked, "Do you mind if I sit here?" I responded, "No." She was a beautiful girl who said that she was from Alaska and that she was going to college in Denver. She said that she was going home for Christmas.

She asked me if I was headed to Vietnam and I told her that I was. She said, "I feel so sorry for you guys that are having to go over there." She asked me if I had a family and I told her that I had a wife and a baby girl. She said, "I will pray for your safety every night." When we landed in Seattle, she hugged me and said, "Be safe."

As we were coming into the civilian airport in Seattle the late afternoon sun was hitting the snow-covered west side of Mt. Rainer. My dad had told me to look for it when I arrived in Seattle if it wasn't cloudy or raining. He was stationed at Fort Lewis right after WWII was over and said that it was cloudy and rained most of the time and you couldn't see the mountains, but that evening it was a beautiful sight to see. The light pink flamingo sunshine hitting the snow on the side of the mountain was beautiful. It amazed me at the size of the mountain.

When we landed military buses were waiting to take all Army personnel to the Fort. They assigned us a bunk and said that we would be woken up at 4:30 a.m. and to check the ship out list that would be put on the bulletin board in the barracks and if your name was on it to report to where it said for you to go with your duffle bag. They said if your name is not on the list, fall out for formation at 4:45 a.m. for duty.

They woke us up at 4:30 a.m. and I checked the ship-out list. Most of the G.I.'s names were on the list, but mine and about ten others were not on the list. They marched the G.I.'s on the list away and had the rest of us got in formation. They told us that we would be assigned K.P. duty for the day. They told me that I was to report to the Company C mess hall at 5:00 a.m. I went into the mess hall and a cook yelled at me to come behind the counter with him. He was getting ready to pour pancakes. He showed me when and how to flip the pan cakes, and the other guy on K.P. when to remove them from the grill. I had never flipped pancakes before, but after a few hundred of them, I got pretty good at it.

After the breakfast meal, we were given pealing knives and told to peel the two sacks of potatoes that were in the room. That was fun! In the afternoon they took me to the big sinks and I washed big pots and pans for the next few hours. I had never had K.P. duty during Basic and AIT training and after this one, I didn't want it again.

I had a small alarm clock in my duffle bag so I dug it out when I got back to the barracks and set it for 4:00 a.m. The next morning, I got up at 4:00 a.m. and put my fatigues on, and quietly walked up to the bulletin board the new list was up and my name was still not on the ship-out list. So, I just left the barracks and walked around the Fort. I went into the mess hall to eat when breakfast was ready and a different one for lunch and dinner. I went to Fort PX and several recreation areas during the day and just looked around. When it was time I went back to the barracks to sleep. There was a whole group of new guys that were there to ship out to Vietnam.

The next morning was the same. My name was still not on the ship-out list. So, I did the same thing as the day before. I thought maybe they have lost my records or something. But the next morning my name was at the top of the ship-out list. We loaded on the buses, and they took us to the airport.

We loaded on the plane and shortly thereafter departed. The pilot came on the intercom and told us that we would be landing in Hawaii, and that we would have an hour layover to refuel, but that we were not to leave the airport terminal.

I finally got tired of looking out the window and thought that I would read something. Back then airplanes had magazines in the pouch in front of your seat. I picked out a Readers Digest to look at. On the front cover, there was a headline that the Vietnam War was almost over and named Cu Chi as an area. Little did I know that I would be headquartered out of Cu Chi. After reading the article I thought, *Good, it's almost over.*

After about two weeks out of Cu Chi, I thought I'll never believe a word in Readers Digest again. What they had written in it was not true.

After leaving Hawaii the pilot said that we would be landing at Wake Island and Guam and that the flight would be a long one. He said that we are going to entertain you with a movie. The stewardess set up a white screen in the front of the cabin and the projector was in the back. The movie that they showed was Camelot.

When we landed at Wake Island and Guam to refuel, we could see all of the old World War II-damaged airplanes that had just been bulldozed off over the edge of the airstrip. We got to disembark at each stop, but it was the same as in Hawaii, we couldn't leave the airport.

Our next stop would be Cam Ranh Bay, South Vietnam. We arrived in Cam Ranh Bay at about 7:00 p.m. As we walked down the plank we could hear artillery explosions on the hills above.

I was now in Vietnam.

★　　★　　★

CHAPTER 5
Arriving in Vietnam

When I arrived in Vietnam at Cam Ranh Bay it was after dark and as we were disembarking the plane we could see and hear artillery rounds hitting the side of a hill in the distance. I remember thinking well I didn't want to go there, but here I am. In all my training I tried to be insignificant and not be noticed, but I thought, now I'm here so I might as well do the best that I can. I decided that I would take my 365 days one day at a time and treat each day as if it would be the only one. Some people counted down on their days and some counted up. I decided that I would count up. A veteran sergeant warned me to be extremely careful during my first and last month in the country because most guys that got killed were in the first or last month of their tour of duty.

They put us up in a metal barrack with screen wire in the upper half of the building. We were told that while we were waiting to be assigned to a unit we would be pulling guard duty along 200 yards of chain link fence with razor wire on the outside of the fence. We were issued M14 rifles like the ones we trained with in basic training. We were issued three loaded magazines for the weapon and were told not to lock and load a magazine unless the base was attacked. On my Christmas Eve guard duty walk there were three groups of soldiers sitting in circles smoking dope out in a field by the fence. They were yelling and hollering at me every time I walked by them. They were all well-spaced out. About the third time I walked by them a large rock came whizzing past my head and I said, "Hey guys, don't throw rocks at me." I just ignored them and walked on. I thought, is this the way troops treat each other over here? The next time I walked by, they didn't throw rocks at me… until I got past them, and then four rocks were thrown at me and one hit me in the back. I thought *That's it, enough!* I turned around and slapped a magazine into the weapon and locked and loaded it. I walked up to them and told them in a stern voice, "The next rock that is thrown at me I'm going to start shooting, you got that?" I turned and resumed my guard duty, and I walked by the drug heads many more times that Christmas Eve night. Guess what, NO more rocks. I walked the same guard duty on Christmas night and the same druggies were there, but they didn't throw any more rocks! I think that they got the message! The day after Christmas they had us fallout in formation and told us that our duty stations had been determined and that we could go to chow and return to the barracks. We were told that when we returned from chow to look on the bulletin board to see what our assignments were. When we returned I looked up my name on the bulletin board and saw that I was assigned to the 25th Infantry Division headquartered in Cu Chi. I was to be in Bravo Company of the 2nd of the 22nd mechanized infantry.

They bused us to the airport at Cam Ranh Bay and I caught a C-130 cargo plane that was flying to Cu Chi. The plane ride to Cu Chi was kind of rough. The plane rattled and shook to Cu Chi. We arrived in Cu Chi at about 3:00 in the afternoon. A jeep driver met us at the airport and he took the three of us that had been assigned to Bravo Company to our company area.

The NCO in charge of the rear area told us that we would be attending a 2-day in-county refresher training course before we were to be sent out in the field.

CHAPTER 6
First Day with Triple Deuce Bravo Company

The insignia on our tracks was a white diamond with a "2" in each corner, and that was the reason that we were called the triple deuce.

After my two days of in-country refresher training, I caught the evening resupply flight out to Bravo Company. I arrived about 4:00 p.m. and the whole company was saddling up with lots of ammo and hand grenades. All the men had a grave look on their faces. The Company Commander gave a short speech and said that we were going back into a small village on the edge of the jungle and that we would conduct a cordon and search mission in the village for VC and weapons.

I asked a squad member why everyone seemed to be so scared and he said that they went into the village the evening before and that they got ambushed and two guys got killed and four were wounded. Now we are going back in. I didn't know what to expect. I grabbed two bandoleers of M16 ammo, each one had seven, twenty-round magazines. Then I put four baseball hand grenades in my pockets, also every man carried a 100-round belt of M60 machine gun ammo either wrapped around his waist or across his chest.

We rode the tracks up to within 400 meters of the village and got off to make a foot assault. When we got close to the village we spread out online about 10 meters apart. Everyone knew where they were to go to encircle the village. On the signal, we all ran as fast as we could to completely cordon off the village. When I got to the edge of the village I dropped down behind a tree and assumed a fighting position. After the circle was complete the captain sent a platoon in the search for VC and weapons. Our job on the perimeter was to make sure that no one escaped.

My squad leader, Sergeant Bob Sachie, told me to hold my position by the tree and I used the tree for cover in case we were hit. The people in the small village ignored us like we weren't even there.

A Vietnamese woman with two small naked boys came up about ten feet from me. She had a small paper sack and a pan of water with her. She took a stick and raked up a small pile of straw. Then she removed 3 big rats from the sack and stuffed them into the straw. She took a box of matches out of her pocket and set the straw on fire. They all squatted around the fire until it burned out. The women then took the burned black rats out of the fire and pinched the feet and tail off and stripped the blackened skin off them. Then she swished them off in the pan of water and handed one to each boy. I watched them eat the rat's bones and all. It was quite a culture shock to me and I thought these people over here are probably having trouble getting something to eat.

After a search of the village turned up with no VC or weapons we returned to our tracks and went back to our logger site for the night. We sent out three eight-man ambushes that night but the Company Commander told me that I wouldn't have to go since it was my first night with the company. That first night I about got eaten alive by the mosquitoes.

★ ★ ★

================================ CHAPTER 7 ================================
First Ambush

When I arrived in Vietnam it was right at the end of the rainy season. It didn't rain every day just occasionally. There was still lots of standing water in many areas. When it did rain, sometimes as the clouds were going away you would get to see the most brilliant, beautiful rainbows. I believe it was because the air was so clean.

On the second night with Bravo Company I was picked to go on one of the three eight-man ambushes. My squad leader Sergeant Bob Sachie was to take out the ambush that I was to go on. Sometimes when you were to go on an ambush it would be with a different squad leader than your own. There was a rotation worked out that you went on an ambush every two out of three nights. The night that you didn't go on an ambush you stayed in the logger site to provide security for the mechanized infantry tracks.

Sergeant Sachie called me aside and told me since you are a FANUGE (which meant something new guy) I'll tell you what to do on ambush. He said, "Stay 10 meters apart when we are moving, if we blow ambush don't fire until I blow my claymore, on the watch don't go to sleep, and questions?" I said, "Yes, how much ammo and stuff should I take?" He told me whatever I wanted except that I was required to take one claymore and one hundred rounds of M60 ammo for the machine gun. Then he told me to get saddled up.

I picked up three, seven-clip bandoleers of M16 ammo, one Claymore mine, four baseball hand grenades, and a hundred-round belt of M60 machine gun ammo. I put my flak jacket, steel pot, and web gear on and picked up my M16. I was ready to go. I didn't know what to expect, but I had noticed in the short time that I had been there that no one was gung-ho about going on nighttime ambushes.

After eating a C-ration meal, it was time to go on the ambush. The tracks fired up and we all jumped on and headed to the staging spot to be dropped off. When we were about 800 meters from our ambush site when the tracks slowed down and Sergeant Sachie said to jump off and hit the ground. All eight of us jumped off the moving tracks and laid down as quickly as possible. After the tracks were gone for a while, we made the defensive circle with everyone facing in. You would watch the eyes of the man across from you and watch behind him. He would do the same with you.

When it started getting dusk dark Sergeant Sachie whispered, "Let's move out." We came out of the wood line into a large opening. We were on the south side of the clearing and the south side and north side both sloped down to the middle of the clearing. We were supposed to ambush a trail on the wood line on the north side of the clearing.

When we got about 1/3 of the way across the opening, we could see a fairly large area of water almost across the middle of the clearing. Sergeant Sachie, who had been there for almost a year was very experienced, but he whispered, "I'm not crossing that water, we'll just set up our ambush here."

From where we set up it was about 300 meters to the wood line on all four sides of us. There were some rice paddy dikes in the area that we set up in and we set up on the west side of a rice paddy dike. We were on full alert until 10:00 p.m. Then one man would be on watch with the starlight scope while the other men slept. We would change every two hours.

I was given the first watch and all the other seven were sacked out. It was a nice calm starlit night, and the starlight scope was picking up good images. I constantly scanned the area in all directions for the first hour and I saw no movement. So, at 11:00 p.m. I called White I, (Captains Track) and reported that this is White 3 and I have a negative Sit-Rap. Sit-Rap was short for situation report if you didn't call in a Sit-Rap on the hour the communications track would call you and say if you can't talk right now push the squelch button twice if the enemy is near and once if everything is okay. After calling in the first Sit-Rap I resumed scanning the area with the starlight scope.

At about 11:30 p.m. I was scanning every direction with the starlight scope. When I looked to the east, I saw movement coming out of the wood line. They came out in the open and I counted twenty of them. Then they spread out about 10 meters apart walking abreast and were coming straight to our ambush position. Sergeant Sachie was asleep on the other end of our line so I woke up the guy that was asleep next to me and told him to low crawl down to Sachie and wake him up. Tell him that I've got movement and that they are coming straight to us. He woke Sergeant Sachie up and he low-crawled up to me and said, "What do you mean that you got movement FANUGY? There are twenty-one of them about 80 meters out still coming straight at us." He said, "Let me see the starlight." He looked for a split second, and said, "V. C., V. C., wake everyone up and get ready! He whispered where everyone could hear him, don't blow your claymore until I blow mine, and then blow it and open up with your weapons on fully auto. Sergeant Sachie stayed next to me and his RTO (radio operation) with the PRICK 25 two-way radio next to him.

They were almost in our kill zone and every one of us had our safety off and turned to full-auto and the clacker of the Claymores in our other hand. I believe that we were about ten seconds from blowing the ambush when I heard the radio squelch and they said, "White 1, White 3 – this is White 1, be advised that the Wolf Hounds, (a straight-leg infantry unit) will be moving through you position shortly – DO NOT FIRE on them! Our RTO man quickly got the Wolf Hounds' call sign and called them and advised them that they were entering a kill zone of our ambush. They answered, "Roger that, DO NOT FIRE on us, we will not fire on you!

They continued into our position and as they walked through, we greeted each other with a "Hi" or a "Hello". I learned something there. A chill came over me when I realized that we almost had a firefight with our men. I thought *We should have been where we were supposed to be.*

After the Wolf Hounds passed through, I finished my watch shift and woke up the next guy and then I went to sleep. At about 5:00 a.m. it was still dark and a squad member woke me up and said that it was my turn to watch again.

I took the starlight and started scanning all around again. About 15 minutes after I went on guard I heard a helicopter fly over. It sounded like it was pretty high and it didn't have any lights on. About 5 minutes later I heard the radio squelch. I answered it and they said, White 3 this is Sunset 6 (sunset 6 was an artillery base) the people sniffer flew over and picked up a reading about 400-meters to you Lima, (the day code word for south) be advised we are going to bust some KJ's on the reading location. KJ's were Killer Junior 155 aerial burst artillery. Tell your people to get their heads down in zero 5 minutes. I woke Sergeant Sachie up and told him what Sunset 6 had said. He woke everyone else up and said, "Everyone gets down as low as you can." Sergeant Sachie was on the radio right beside me when the artillery unit said, "Hang It" which meant that the shell was leaving the gun and on its way. They would say splash as the round was about to explode. When they said splash the round exploded right over our head, and the concussion and shell fragments rocked us on the ground. Immediately Sergeant Sachie yelled on the radio, Sunset 6, Sunset 6, this is White 3, cease fire, cease fire, that's us, that's us! After a short delay, they came back on the radio and said, Roger that. We whispered loud is anybody hit? Everyone answered NO. It was a miracle that none of us were hit. When it became daylight, we could see big holes in the ground all around us from the shrapnel impact.

A lesson that I learned, again and I never forgot later when I became squad leader, platoon sergeant, and acting platoon leader, always be where you are supposed to be, water or no water. The people sniffer reading was us because we weren't where we were supposed to be. It is a miracle that none of us were wounded or killed on my first ambush.

★　　★　　★

CHAPTER 8

First Dead VC

My second ambush was on a well-used trail, but we never saw any enemy personnel. My third ambush was different!

A typical 8-man ambush consisted of a sniper with a silencer and starlight scope, a troop with an M79 Grenade launcher and 80 rounds in his vest, an M60 machine gunner, and five with M-16s and one of those was the R.T.O. man (radio man). The machine gunner carried 200 rounds and everybody else carried a 100-round belt for the M60. All squad members carried a claymore mine, (a curved mine with spikes at the bottom to stick in the ground). There were 700 steel balls imbedded in the C-4 explosive of the mines and they were set off by a clacker that you pushed three times quickly to set off. The soldiers with M16s usually carried 2 bandoleers of seven 20-round mags, which was 14 magazines. I always carried 3 bandoleers or twenty-one 20-round mags. Some guys only carried one hand grenade, but I always carried four, and sometimes six. The squad leader would also carry a strobe light to direct helicopters to our position, and two smoke flares for position marking in the daytime.

A typical ambush would consist of a platoon of four mechanized infantry tracks on a roving patrol late in the evening. They would take you usually within 200 to 300 meters of your ambush site. They wouldn't stop and we would jump off and hide as they moved on out and back to the company's logger site. We would then find a fairly hidden place and sit in a small circle facing in so that we could watch the soldier's eyes that were across from us. We would stay there in complete silence until it was just dark enough to see silhouettes, and then we would move into our ambush site and set up as quickly as possible.

We were still sitting in our circle facing in and I was watching behind the guys in front of me. The trooper straight across from me had the M79 grenade launcher. All of a sudden, he got this crazy weird look on his face and he pointed his grenade launcher at me. I remember thinking has he gone crazy and is he going to shoot me with it? He raised his aim over my head and pulled the trigger. The round went right over my head, and then a loud explosion. About 15 meters behind me. I rolled over and looked. There was a stump about 4-foot-tall 15 meters behind me and a VC with an RPG over his shoulder jumped up on the stump and started looking around, and that is when my squad member shot him with the M79 grenade.

We waited a while in full alert and no other enemy showed, so we crawled over to look at the VC The round hit him somewhere between his left shoulder and his neck and it completely blew his left shoulder, arm, and head completely off. That was the first death of many that I was to see, and I remember thinking… People are killing people over here!

★ ★ ★

==== **CHAPTER 9** ====
Facing Death

It has been said many times that "War is Hell" Anyone who has been in combat knows what that means. How do you face fear and how do you face the possibility of death or severe injury? There are many ways that soldiers find to face these dangers. You must make peace with yourself and peace with God. One of the things that gave me the courage to face the possibility of death or severe injury was the Psalm. It went something like this: "The Lord is my shepherd, I shall not want, he maketh me lie down in green pastures, he leadeth me beside the still waters, he restoreth my soul for his namesake, and yea though I walk through the valley of the shadow of death, I shall fear no evil, for thy are with me, thy rod and thy staff they comfort me, surely goodness and mercy shall follow me all the days of my life, and then I shall dwell in the house of the Lord forever." I would say a silent prayer when things looked bad. "Lord, if I am supposed to die here, please let it be quick." The weapons that I carried were to me my rod and my staff that comforted me – my M16 and my 1911 45-caliber pistol were them.

Many people react in different ways to fear. Terror is hearing a mortar round hit the bottom of the tube and hearing it go up and then you could hear it sizzling down, with no idea where it was going to hit. In a firefight, our training would automatically take over and if you could make it to the ground you had a good chance of not getting killed. In a firefight, I always had this cool, calm feeling come over me, and everything became so clear and vivid. The only thing that mattered was that minute, that second, right there. It is hard to explain that feeling unless you have been there yourself. The feeling that you have after combat is you hate it, the smell of gunpowder and fresh dirt and sometimes the smell of blood, but after a while you kind of get to liking it. It's hard to explain how you could hate something and still like it. The only way I could justify that feeling was that it must be the adrenaline rush.

Everyone was always scared in combat, but most people were able to function and overcome that fear. What I have learned is that there is no motivator like FEAR! Fear can be good; it can help you make good common-sense decisions that lead to good outcomes. A full Bird Colonel was giving a speech when he was presenting me with a metal for Valor, and he said, "Well, what you did was just good common sense!" He then paused for a while and said, "Although all too often, I find that common sense is not that common anymore."

Our training helped us to overcome our fear. The Army would tear you down in basic training and then they would build you up to make you think that you were almost invisible. I still remember parts of our training like the drill sergeant that trained us in survival and said, "Every tree is cover, every rock is cover, every hill is cover, every blade of grass is cover, and last, every man is cover." One thing about fear is that you must know fear before you know what it is to be brave.

CHAPTER 10
Thoughts of a Soldier

I often wondered when I was in Vietnam what power one man has over another to make him kill other people that he didn't want to kill. Part of this was to dehumanize the people that they wanted you to kill by calling them V. C, or Charlie. We only killed when we had to for each other and to try and stay alive. The personal objective for you to achieve was to try to stay alive for 365 days or all your tour of duty no matter how long it was. The training that we received in basic and advanced infantry training was very good and when something happened you would automatically respond without thinking. After you had killed some Viet Cong or North Vietnam Army Troops you had a sort of sickening feeling and you would think to yourself, that he was some momma's baby boy. The only thing that bothered me was that even though you hated it, the smell of gunpowder, fresh dirt, blood, and death, you kind of got used to it. The only way that I could justify that double feeling was to blame it on an adrenalin rush.

For some reason, I always got a cool, calm feeling during a fire-fight. It is hard to explain it, but you had an intense feeling that the only thing that mattered was that second, that minute, that hour, and day. Nothing else was on your mind; you and your senses were present. That was the only thing that mattered.

I thought that no one knows what infantrymen go through other than the ones who have been there. It seemed like no one that hadn't been there or had a relative at home cared what you had gone through and what you had done.

I had killed people and saw people killed and wounded, and I had been wounded myself. I had slept on the ground in the monsoons when the water was six inches deep. I had lived through the dry season when the heat, the dust, and the mosquitos were almost unbearable, and I had been away from my family for a long period.

Someone once asked me, "Where were your barracks when you were in Vietnam?" The ground was mostly our barracks was my answer. I thought, for all the things that I have done, as the saying went among fighting men in Vietnam when something happened that didn't cost life or limb, "It Doesn't Mean Nothing."

CHAPTER 11

Doc Adams

Every platoon in our infantry company had a medic. Most of them were very good at their job. Most of the medics were conscientious objectors and were opposed to killing. When they were assigned to a unit, they were not issued a weapon. But every one of the medics except one would ask for an M16 when the going got tough.

Our third platoon medic was from a small town in Kansas, and we called him Doc Adams. When I got hit in the leg, I was his first patient. He was shaking so badly that I had to put the bandage on myself. He went on to be the best medic in our unit, and no matter how bad the situation got he would not pick up a weapon.

We had a soldier that got hit in the chest and had a sucking chest wound, I helped Doc Adams seal the wound with plastic and tape to keep his lungs from collapsing. We dusted him off as soon as we could. Doc Adams went with him on the chopper. Doc returned the next day on the resupply helicopter and told us that the wounded man was going to make it. Doc Adams turned out to be a very good medic and saved several GI's lives.

CHAPTER 12
The People of Vietnam

I met many of the Vietnamese people while I was in Vietnam. I was impressed with the intelligence of the people. Even those out in the countryside that were living as the Vietnamese people had probably lived for centuries were impressive.

The impression that I got from them was that most of them just wanted to be left alone. They were mostly self-sufficient farmers, and of course, rice was the main crop that they grew. I was amazed at the productivity that they had as farmers because I didn't see any mechanized farm equipment. All the work was done by hand or by a water buffalo pulling a wooden plow.

I was told that not all kids got to attend school. That only the well-to-do and politicians' children were usually the only ones that got to attend school.

All the Vietnamese people that I saw were always out early working in their fields or paddy's or trying in some way to get food. There were no welfare or food stamps in their country, so if you didn't work you didn't eat.

The Vietnamese Chu Hoi scouts that were the enemy and then came over to our side were very impressive people. They would be sent to a three-week course in English and at the end of the course they could pretty well communicate with you in English. I don't believe that I could learn Vietnamese enough to talk to them the way the scouts could talk to us in just three weeks. Some of the Vietnamese words and phrases that we did learn, mostly out of necessity were:

lai – dai = come here
chu – hoi = surrender, give up
dong – li = stop
di di mau = go away, leave, get
eu – bic = you understand
hooch = house
crackadol = kill

These were the only Vietnamese words that we had to know to relatively get by.

★ ★ ★

CHAPTER 13
Typical Day in Vietnam

I f you were on one of the three, eight-man ambushes that Bravo Company sent out every night you would come back to the logger site at about 8:00 a.m. Some mornings the choppers would fly out a hot breakfast of powdered scrambled eggs, sausage, one piece of toast, and a glass of Tang. All the other mornings we would eat C-rations. Then we would break the logger site and go on a daytime search and destroy mission. Sometimes the missions were mounted ones where we stayed on the APCs, sometimes they were roving patrols on foot and sometimes we went on Eagle flights. Four Huey helicopters would pick up my platoon and drop us off in an area we were to search and then we would walk to our next objective and then the chopper would pick us up and return us to our new logger site around 4:00 p.m.

We would set up the tracks in a circle like covered wagons. Every squad would go to work quickly and set up an RPG screen in front of each track, dig two M60 machine gun fighting positions, one on each side of the track, set out two rows of claymore mines, and way out front set out one or two rows of trip flares. Each platoon would also send one man to the center of the logger side to help dig a garbage sump for any trash that we may have. The next morning, they would cover the hole back up.

The ambushes would go out about one hour before dark and the troops that were left in the logger site would have 100% alert until 10:00 p.m. and one man on guard on top of each mechanized track until one hour before daylight and then we went back to 100% alert. The ambushes generally had the same times of alerts, but if the squad leader determined that they were in a really bad dangerous area there would be 100% alert all night, which meant no sleep.

After 8:00 a.m. all three ambushes would walk back in, and we would break the logger site and start on whatever mission that we were assigned for that day.

★ ★ ★

Eagle Flight

About once or twice a week during the day, instead of going on track-mounted search and destroy missions or foot patrol we would go on what was called Eagle Flight. An eagle flight was when four Huey helicopters would arrive and pick up my platoon and take us to a predetermined location. The side doors were open on both sides of the helicopter, and we would sit on the edge with our legs dangling out. There was a door gunner on each side of the helicopter with an M60 machine gun with butterfly triggers, which meant that you fired them with both thumbs. The first time I was on an eagle flight when the helicopter banked with us on the low side, I thought that we were going to fall out because there was nothing to hold on to. Someone said we're going to fall out, and the door gunner yelled, "You won't fall out the pressure will keep you in."

As a platoon sergeant, I was given a map with objectives to go to, also a list with the compass courses, and the number of meters from the drop zone to the objectives. We would look for VCs, bunkers, and tunnels. We had to be very aware of booby traps or ambushes.

The helicopters would drop us off and we would walk to our objective and then call them to come and pick us up. They would then take us to our next objective the same way all day.

When the helicopters dropped us off they would never land. They would hover about 8 to 10 feet above the ground, and yell "JUMP!" They would drop us in some type of clearing every time and you didn't know if you would be jumping into a hot L.Z. or not.

During the rainy season, the helicopter pilots would always drop us off in the water. When you jumped from the choppers to the water you never knew how deep you were going to go. They did this because the VC and NVA had developed booby traps for helicopters. The type that they had consisted of a firing device that was triggered with a propeller to pull the pen on the booby trap. They would try to predetermine where a helicopter would land and set them there.

As the helicopters landed the prop blast from the blades would wind the propeller on the booby trap and the chord would wrap around an object and pull the pin on it setting it off. The helicopter pilots that I worked with were very good. We didn't blame them for dropping us in water or exposed areas because of the possibility of these types of booby traps. When they dropped us off on eagle flights they would get out of the area as fast as they could to keep from getting hit with rocket-propelled grenades or as we called them RPGs.

CHAPTER 15

Wounded in Action

We moved to a new larger site about 12 miles northeast of Cu Chi, which was our big base of operation. The area was in what was called "The Iron Triangle." We called it the "fill hole" because that was what the guys that had been there almost a year nicknamed it.

The area was a patchwork of the jungle, bamboo hedgerows, plowed clear areas that were grown up in brush that was waist to head high. We set up our logger site about ¾-mile from the Saigon River, which was to our east.

The area we set up in was a large fairly open area about ½-mile square, with a swag in the middle. To our north and our south was slightly uphill. We sent out three ambushes that night, and I was on the one that went to the south. In the other two ambushes, one went to the north and one to the east toward the river.

We had a routine ambush and none of the three ambushes had any enemy movement, so we walked back in. Our third squad ambush was the first one back to the logger site. Just as we arrived, we heard a chopper coming. It was a resupply chopper, and it also had a hot breakfast on board for us. They landed and the two cooks on board set up a chow line with haste. The meal consisted of bacon, powdered scrambled eggs, one piece of toast, and Tang. We only got these hot meals about once a week and sometimes once every two weeks.

Just as we lined up with our mess kits to go through the food line. The 2nd platoon ambush came in and quickly got in line for the chow. As I was going through the chow line I looked to the north and I saw the 1st platoon ambush working their way down the slope. All of a sudden, I saw them hit the ground and dust was flying up all around them. Then I heard the gunfire. We dropped our mess kits, grabbed our weapons, and jumped on the tracks to go help them. The company commander had our 20 tracks spread out on the line and swept into the area. The VC had broken contact when they heard the tracks coming. When we got to the 1st platoon of guys, we were amazed that no one was hit! We turned toward the Saigon River, and we started jumping VCs. They would jump up, fire their AK-47, and then run. We were on top of our tracks and when one would run we would mow him down. We killed several VCs. our CO believed that a whole company of VCs was spread out in the area. He stopped our movement and called in a wall of 155mm artillery to our front and our left. The Saigon River was to the right. The river at that point was about 700 meters wide. We had them trapped on three sides and we were on the fourth side. He ordered us to move out. The track drivers roared their diesel engines and moved out in unison. VC started jumping, firing, and running in front of us. We were receiving fire, but we were delivering devastating fire on them. I was firing my M16 and changing magazines as fast as I could. I was setting on the right side of the track and the main hatch lid was open. Just as I started firing again three VCs jumped to run while firing back at us and the track to my right hit a mine. Something hit me on my left calf and spun me around and I fell inside the open hatch of the track.

Sergeant Sachie heard me hit the floor and yelled at me, "Get back up on top!" I said, "I'm hit!" He said, "What!" I said, "I'm hit in my leg." He said, "Oh, I didn't know!" He stopped the track and jumped down to help me. They opened the back hatch and got me out on the ground, and he yelled for the medic. The medic was a conscientious objector from Pee Body, Kansas and I was his first patient. He was shaking so badly that he couldn't put the bandage on me. I had to put it on myself. He turned out later to be the best medic that we had. He was the only conscientious objector that would not touch a weapon when the stuff got bad. All the others would grab a weapon when things looked bad.

The CO called in a dust-off for me, and he told me it would be there in about 15 minutes. At about 10 minutes he received a call from the dust-off pilot asking if I could wait about 30 minutes because he had another very life-threatening call. The CO asked me if I could make it for thirty more minutes and I said "Yes." In about 30 minutes, he came back and picked me up, and flew me to the hospital at Cu Chi. Two young doctors went to work on my leg. They had me on my stomach and gave me shots all around the wound to numb it. They told me that they would have to clean out the debride and damaged tissue and try to remove the projectile. They worked on me for about 20 minutes, and I could hear them whispering to each other. Then they went and got the head doctor to come to look at my wound. He came around in front of me and he said, "We have a problem!"! He said, "The projectile is right against the main nerve in your leg. If we take it out, there is a possibility that you could lose the feeling from there down permanently. What do you want us to do?" My mind raced, and I thought how can I make this decision on such short notice? So, I told the doctor, "I'm going to ask you a question and don't lie to me. What would you do if it was you?" He said, "If it was me, I would leave it." So I said, "Leave it"! I was in the hospital for two days and in the company area in Cu Chi for three more days and they sent me back to the field. I still couldn't walk very well on my left leg.

While I was in the company area in Cu Chi 1ˢᵗ Sergeant Tinga yelled, "Private Whalen you have a visitor", and I thought, how could I have a visitor? When he came in, he was with Master Sergeant Sanders. I had coached his son in Salina just a year before. He stayed for about 30 minutes and then shook my hand and told me to get well soon. About 15 minutes later Top yelled again Private Whalen you have another visitor. It was a soldier, Larry Cousatte, from my county seat town, Pryor, Oklahoma. He said he saw my name on the casualties' board, and that he was going home, and he would find my wife and let her know that he had seen me and that I was going to be alright. He went home and found my wife in the Post Office, he was in his uniform, and asked her if she was Mike Whalen's wife… She told me later that her heart just dropped. I guess he saw the look on her face and he said, "No, no I saw him, he's going to be all right." After Larry Cousatte left me First Sergeant Tinga yelled again, "Private Whalen you have another visitor."

When my next visitor walked in I couldn't believe it. It was my third cousin, Randy Jetton. He was a civilian engineer that lived in Manila and flew back and forth from Manila to Vietnam every day. He had also seen my name on the wounded in the action list. He had his jeep, and he said let's go for a ride, grab your crutches, and jump in. We drove around in the Cu Chi base for a while and he got on the main road that headed for the main gate. When we got close to the gate I said, "We're not going outside the berm, are we?" He said, "Yea, let's go for a ride out in the country." I said, "We don't even have a M16!" He said, "They won't bother you in the daytime!" We drove through two small villages and then to the south end of a big clearing with four trees out in the middle. I said, "Do you see those trees out there? I was on an ambush out there one week ago and we got ambushed, and we had one man killed." I said, "I think we better get back to Cu Chi," he agreed. When we returned, he said, "I'll keep checking on you and he left to fly back to Manila."

CHAPTER 16
800 Man NVA Battalion Ambush

It was my first night back with Bravo Company after I was released from the hospital after I was wounded in the leg. Captain Pensky sent for me to come to his track in the logger site. I reported to him and he said for me to take the night off of going on ambush since it was my first night back. I asked him who was taking out the ambush the next night and he said it would be Sergeant Poatas. I asked him, who is Poatas? He said, "We got him while you were gone." He is a graduate of NCO school. It is his first time taking out an ambush. We called sergeants who got their stripes in NCO school, "Shake and Bake or Jiffy Pop sergeants" Most sergeants got their stripes after about six or seven months of combat experience, I asked Captain Pensky, who is taking out the 3rd platoon ambush tonight? He said Sergeant Fairbanks and I had walked point for him several times. He knew his stuff. The best compliment that a leader could get from platoon members was that he's got his crap together, and if you ask what that meant, they would say, "Five pounds of crap in a one-pound can."

So I asked Captain Pensky if I could go tonight and take tomorrow night off. He said, "Whichever you want to do is fine with me." So I said I would go with Fairbanks. I went to Fairbanks and told him that I would be going on his ambush tonight. He said okay, will you walk point for me? I knew that he trusted me because of the times I had walked point for him before. He told me to go get saddled up and that we were leaving in 20 minutes. I grabbed three bandoleers of M16 ammo which was 21, twenty-round magazines, a 100-round belt of M60 machine gun ammo, one Claymore mine, and four baseball hand grenades.

When we were all ready to go the sniper who was to go with us came down with diarrhea and had to drop out. All the nighttime ambushes usually consisted of eight men. Tonight it would be a seven-man ambush. We had one man with an M79 grenade launcher with sixty rounds for his weapon and a good machine gunner with an M60 machine gun. He carried the gun and four, one hundred round belts of ammunition. Our machine gunner was from Texas. So of course, everybody called him Tex. Tex was an easy-going laid-back personality, but in a firefight, he would lay down a heavy base of the fire. Another man with an M16 also carried the PRICK-25 radio for our communications. The rest of us carried M-16s and 21, twenty-round magazines of ammo. Everyone carried one Claymore command detonated mine, a hundred-round belt of M60 ammo, and ever how many hand grenades you wanted to carry. I believe in hand grenades, so I usually carried a minimum of four and up to as many as eight if I thought that we were in a pretty bad area. We would hear stories of some of Charlie company's ambushes being overrun by the enemy and I thought that if it was to happen to us the extra hand grenades would come in handy. The baseball-type grenades weighed four pounds each so you could get weighted down by carrying several of them.

The third platoon's mechanized infantry tracks fired up and we headed to our staging area to be dropped off about three hundred meters from our ambush site. All the platoon members were on the tracks except the ones that were going on a different ambush. The tracks would not stop when we arrived at our staging area. When Sergeant Fairbanks gave the signal all seven of the ambush members jumped off while the tracks were still moving the rest of the platoon members stayed with the APCs for security. The tracks would make a big circle and return to the logger site for the night.

When we jumped off the tracks we would quickly hide and set up in a circle with everyone facing the center of the circle. You watched behind the troop that you were facing and you watched his eyes.

When it was dusky dark Sergeant Fairbanks told me to move out. He had shown me on the map where we were supposed to go. I took the point and the other six spread out about ten meters apart. Sergeant Fairbanks was the next guy behind me and then his RTO man. Tex was next with the M60 machine gun and behind him was our M79 grenade launcher man, and the last three had M16s.

When you walked point you did it at your own pace. You had to look for anything out of the ordinary, and movement, any ground disturbance, or trip wires. I walked point as if I was still hunting for deer. My dad had taught me how to be still and hunt. He showed me that you take three steps and stop for six, while you surveil the surroundings for any kind of movement. He told me that you must see them before they see you. It was good advice and it worked well for me anytime that I walked point.

We had moved about 200 meters when I approached a large clearing that was about the size of a football field. It had thin bamboo hedge rows around the edges of the field. Before I moved through the thin hedge row I stopped and scanned the field and the surrounding area. I didn't see anything, so I stepped out onto the edge of the opening. Just as I stepped out, I saw two NVA soldiers walking abreast on the other end of the field. I dropped to the ground as fast as I could and watched them through the foot-tall grass. I didn't know if they had seen me or not. When I hit the ground all the men behind me hit the ground too. Sergeant Fairbanks low crawled up to me and whispered, "What is it?" I said two NVA in full dress uniform crossed the short end of the field. I don't think they saw me because they kept walking across at the same pace. They were quickly walking across in the opposite direction that I was in. Sergeant Fairbanks said, "They were on the trail that we are supposed to ambush."

About that time as we were peering through the grass two more NVA walking abreast came out and were quickly walking across the field. Fairbanks motioned for the RTO man to bring up the radio. He got Captain Pensky on the horn and said, "We have movement before we got to our ambush site." At about that time, two more NVA entered the field. He told the captain that we have visual on NVA now, "Do you want us to blow the ambush?" He said, "No, wait until you don't see any more and move into your ambush site and set up." The trail that the NVA was on was the one that we were supposed to ambush. As we waited for it to get dark a total of ten NVA crossed the field. We noticed that they had their AK47 strung across their chests.

It was almost dark when we started to move out. Sergeant Fairbanks said to me, "If it's all right with you, I'll take point." I told him it was fine with me because I trusted him and his experience. We scattered out in a 10-meter apart formation. It was just dark enough that you could see silhouettes. My leg was still pretty sore from my wound, and I was walking with a limp. Fairbanks was on point, his radio man behind him, then me, Tex with the M60, and the other four were behind him. We were almost across the field and everyone was looking all around for the enemy. I looked to my left, then forward, then to the right the way the NVA that we had observed had gone. When I looked back to my left I saw Fairbanks and his RTO had disappeared. I knew that they had seen something and had hit the ground. I immediately hit the ground and all the guys behind hit the dirt.

I started looking for what made Fairbanks and his RTO hit the ground. I looked to my right the way the other NVA had gone and

I didn't see anything, then I looked to my left and I couldn't believe what I saw. There were large groups of NVA walking in parade formation coming down the trail. I immediately thought the 10 NVA that we observed earlier were just the point element. The cart path trail made about a 50-meter right turn to the right of Fairbanks and then turned right again and came straight to me. When I hit the ground at first I didn't realize that I was right on the edge of the trail. Then I thought, I'm in trouble. They will step on me. The thought hit me that we are all dead! They were marching at a quick pace, and it wouldn't be long before they were on me. I could see the silhouettes of eight formations. They were walking five abreast and twenty deep. Just as they were about to turn the corner toward me, I thought that our only chance was the M60 machine gun. I turned around and looked at Tex to make sure he was ready and I saw that he had the gun pointed in the other direction. He didn't see them! He later told me that he thought that we saw the other NVA coming back. Just as the point element was turning the corner toward me. I thought I've got to get Tex's attention. I softly said, "Tex." He didn't hear me. I said, "Tex" again a little louder and he still didn't hear me. So I said it again in a really loud whisper. I saw him turn to look at me and I put one arm up where he could see and motioned three times in the direction of the NVA battalion. When he saw them, he just jerked the gun around and made some clanking noise when the ammo belt struck the side of the gun.

The point formation of the NVA battalion soldiers heard me and Tex make the noise and they stopped marching. I could hear them talking and I figured that they were deciding what to do. While they were stopped the formations behind them were stacking up to their rear. While they were talking my training started to take over. We were trained to not cluster up because one burst of automatic fire can kill all of you. I thought that was a cluster-up if I ever saw one. I eased a hand grenade out of my shirt pocket and pulled the pin, and then I thought what am I doing they heard us and they are looking for something to shoot. I thought I'll have to get up on my knees to throw the grenade and they will probably cut me down. So, I fumbled around in the fading light and got the pin back in the grenade. I then put my M16 up where I could barely see the tall front sight and lowered it into the middle of the leading formation. I thought maybe they will go around us, but all at once here they came. I thought somebody do something, somebody do something, they are going to step on me. When they were getting very close, I thought, *it's going to have to be me.* I opened up with a 20-round burst on fully automatic and then all six of the other members of the ambush squad opened up. I fired two magazines on fully automatic and flipped the selector switch to semi-auto on the third one. As I rolled over to slap my fourth magazine in, I looked toward Sergeant Fairbanks and in the muzzle flashes, I could see him up on one knee firing his weapon. I could see green tracers flying all around him. The enemy tracers are green and ours are red. I yelled at him, "Greg, get down!" In the muzzle flashes, I saw him hit the ground. I resumed firing and the enemy shifted their fire from Greg to me. Greg yelled, "Mike, get down!" and that little mound of dirt I was behind came in handy. I got behind the mound and got as low as I could get. I could hear rounds hitting all around me and hitting the dirt mound in front of me. After what seemed like ten minutes, but was probably one, they shifted their fire away from me I resumed firing my M16. As I rolled over on my side to put in a new magazine in the muzzle flashes, I could see silhouettes of NVA running between us in every direction that I looked. We later found out that intelligence predicted that a fresh battalion of Green NVA Troops would enter Vietnam from Cambodia that night and would travel down the trail that we were on. They were green troops and this was their first combat. I believe that our being spread out 10 meters apart is why we survived because they thought we were a much larger force than we were.

Everyone was firing their weapons as fast as they could to try to gain fire superiority as we were trained to do. Between changing magazines, I heard Tex whisper loud "I'm out." I pitched him my 100-round belt and the guy on the other side pitched him the belt that he was carrying. Shortly after that Tex resumed firing his M60 in 3 to 5-round bursts. The troop with the M79 grenade launcher laid on his back and fired up like a motor all around us. He fired them as fast as he could. Most of the rounds that he fired were bouncing Bettys that would hit the ground and bounce up five meters and then explode. They had a kill zone of fifteen meters, were ground impact grenades only had a kill zone of five meters. He later said that he fired forty of the sixty rounds that he carried on his vest. I believe that he had a large impact on all of us surviving that night.

After I had fired eight magazines we stopped receiving return fire. We all low crawled over to Sergeant Fairbanks's position. He and his RTO had found a small bomb crater to get in for cover. We all piled into the crater and made a circle facing out in all directions. Everyone was whispering to each other "we are dead" if they regroup and attack us we don't have a chance. Fairbanks was on the radio with the captain and he told him that the company was on the tracks and on the way and they should be there in fifteen to twenty minutes. We all laid our magazines and grenades out so that we could grab them fast if we were attacked.

The guys that hadn't given their machine gun belts to Tex before gave them to him and he snapped the belts into a 400-round string and stacked them in order so that they wouldn't jam. The captain then asked Sergeant Fairbanks if we had any friendly KIAs or WIAs. Fairbanks told him that is a negative. Then he asked if there were any enemy WIAs or KIAs and Fairbanks said "That is a positive". The captain said for us to get down because Ariel's parachute illumination from 155 artilleries was on the way. Then he said when the illumination is up, send out a killer team and check for bodies. I was lying beside Sergeant Fairbanks and listening to the radio and Fairbanks looked at me and I thought "I'm the killer team." He said, "Mike will you go with me?" I said, "Yea I'll go." I learned a lot from Sergeant Fairbanks about being a leader. Don't ask your men to do something that you wouldn't do yourself. We instructed the other five men to not fire at anything while we were out there. About that time the parachute flair popped over our heads and we started low crawling out. The area was lit up like a Friday night football field. We crawled for about 40 meters in the foot-to-two-foot-tall grass. Fairbanks said, "Okay, let's look". We slowly raised to our knees and looked up and we couldn't see anything. He said, "Nope don't see any." As we were crawling back in the illumination flair went out.

We settled into our positions and got very quiet so that we could listen for any movement. I started hearing small metallic clanks and ticks. I whispered, "Did you hear that?" About that time another click and the other guys whispered I hear it and they all whispered, they are crawling in on us. We kept hearing the ticks and clicks and I whispered to Sergeant Fairbanks I'm going to frag them. He said, "Go ahead." Just after I pulled the pen and started to throw it, he grabbed my arm and said, "Don't throw it, it might give our position away." So I fiddled around in the dark and got the pen back in the hand grenade. Just as I got the pen back in there was a loud metallic click and he whispered, "Throw it, throw it." I pulled the pen again and threw it and whispered, "Frag out." A hand grenade is supposed to go off 3 seconds after the handle pops. Everyone was down as we waited for the explosion. I was counting the seconds and at five one of the guys whispered, "Whalen you forgot to pull the pin" and I whispered back "The pull ring is still on my finger." About that time a couple of guys said, DUD! We all rose and then it went off. The concussion put us all back down in the crater. Shortly after that, we heard the tracks coming. When the company arrived more artillery illumination popped overhead and the captain had the tracks spread out the line, and had everyone but the 50-gunner and driver dismount and spread out so that we could sweep the area. We started sweeping the area and we found several V. C. bodies and numerous blood trails. One guy in the second platoon suddenly gave an automatic burst toward the ground and he said "That V. C. was alive". We also found a lot of drag marks in the grass where they had dragged bodies away. We also found a lot of rifle slings lying in the grass. When the NVA troops were marching in formation they had their AKs slung across their chests. The metallic clicks and clinks that we had heard were them unbuckling the slings from the bodies to take their weapons with them as they left.

After sweeping the area the captain told us to return to our ambush site and set up. We were hoping that he would let us go back into the logger site with them, but that wasn't to be. We set out our claymore mines and got ready for what we thought would probably be a human wave assault. Before the tracks left, we all resupplied ourselves with plenty of ammo and grenades. We had a hundred present alert all night expecting an attack, but it never came. At 8:00 the next morning, we picked up our claymores and walked back to the logger site.

When we arrived at the site one of the soldiers in the second platoon yelled, "Look, there is the magnificent seven!" The only reason that we think of for the NVA not assaulting us was that they had orders for a specific mission and that they didn't want to get side-tracked from that mission.

For our actions, Sergeant Fairbanks and I both received medals for valor. The text reads: Private First Class Whalen, Michael R. of Company B 2nd Battalion, 22nd Infantry metal with "V" devise for valor, heroism in connection with military operations against a hostile force: Private First Class Whalen distinguished himself by heroic actions on March 8, 1970, while serving with Company B, 2nd Battalion, 22nd Infantry in the Republic of Vietnam. While on a reconnaissance operation, elements of Company B encountered a large enemy force. With complete disregard for his safety, Private Whalen exposed himself to a hail of enemy fire as he placed devastating fire on the hostile force. His valorous actions contributed immeasurably to the success of the mission. Private Whalen's bravery and devotion to duty are in keeping with the highest traditions of military service and reflect great credit upon himself, his unit, the 25 Infantry Division, and the United States Army.

CHAPTER 17
The Rock Ambush

The rainy season was just getting underway, and we were changing from dust to mud. The temperature during the day would be around 100 degrees and by 4:00 p.m. the rain would come in for about one to three hours and then the wind would get up and the temperature would drop to about 65 degrees. Between being soaking wet and the big temperature drop your teeth would chatter and you would almost get hypothermia. When we went on ambush during the rainy season everyone would pack a wool army blanket, and you would double up with one of your squad members and put one blanket on the ground and cover up with the other one.

We were on the ambush in an area where a week before we had a major fight with an NVA unit. We were very cautious and afraid because of that. We moved into our ambush site right at dark and set up. I laid my blanket on the ground and my buddy kept his for us to cover up with when we would get our turn to sleep. There was a big rock under my blanket, and I complained about it. When I was up on watch my buddy tried to sleep on my blanket and cover with his. When I woke the next guy up for his turn to watch I went back to my blanket and my blanket mate said, "Man, that rock is killing my back!" We were up one hour before daylight for 100% alert.

No VC or NVA showed up, so we were preparing to go back into the company's logger site when I picked up my blanket and looked at the rock. It was not a rock, but an 82mm mortar round with a hand grenade pull fuse screwed at the end of it. It had an open diaper pen through the pull trigger with a trip wire tied to it. The pin was rusted in place, and we looked at each other and realized how lucky we were that the pin didn't pull! A chill went down my spine as to how close a call that was.

CHAPTER 18
Sergeant Poatas' Death

About two weeks after we blew the ambush on a whole battalion of NVA troops we were moved to an area South of Cu Chi. The area had large areas of rice patties, areas of brush that were overhead high, and some areas of large trees. There were several houses in the area, and some ARVIN compounds (South Vietnamese Army)

The ARVINs were not very good fighters. They lived in their compounds with their families and would hardly ever come out to engage the enemy. We often wondered why the VC and NVA were such good fighters and the ARVINs were not. The only good South Vietnamese troops we worked with were their special forces elite troops. They were good fighters.

We sent out three, eight-man ambushes the first night that we were in the new area south of Cu Chi. Sergeant Poatas, my squad leader, Greg Fairbanks, the second squad leader, and Greg Cannon the first squad's squad leader each took out an eight-man ambush.

I learned another lesson again, "About things not to do that night." Be where you are supposed to be and go where you are supposed to go. Our ambushes that night were on trails that were only about 200 meters apart. So the squad leaders got together and decided that they would all come together that night and have a 24-man ambush so that everyone could get more sleep than normal.

The squad leaders set a time to meet at a place where two trails crossed and then go set up on one of the ambush sites. At the time we usually moved from our staging area to our ambush site we went to the cross-site instead of our ambush site. Then we all moved to the site that the first squad was supposed to ambush.

The ambush site was out in the middle of a one-half-mile square area of rice patties. There was a fairly high patty with five big trees around the edge where the ambush was set up. The trees were the only ones in the whole rice patty area berm. To the south of us in the wood line, there were several houses and in the southwest corner, there was an ARVIN compound. The patty we set up in was not very big and we scattered out and around the inside of the square. We were set up only about three meters apart from each other all around the patty.

Sergeant Poatas told me to take charge of my side of the berm, which was the eastside, and to have the men start setting out claymores while he crossed to the west side where there wasn't a squad leader to get the guys on that side to start putting out their claymores. It was dark enough that you could only see silhouettes of the men out in front of you.

I handed the starlight scope to one member of the squad and the end of my detonator wire for my claymore to another guy to hold while I crawled out to set up my claymore. We did that because if the man with the starlight saw anything they were to jerk three times on the cord, and you were to come back ASAP!

When I got back from setting out my claymore, I held the wire for all the other guys while they set there's out. When the last man was still out I could tell that he was almost through setting out his claymore. While I was holding the cords for the guys I also laid all of my hand grenades and my M16 magazines all in a neat row where I could acquire them rapidly if I needed them. For some reason, I had decided to carry six baseball hand grenades that night.

I could see the silhouette of the private that was the last man on my side to put out his mine. He was a "FANUGY" meaning a guy that hadn't been in the country long and hadn't been in a firefight yet. He was a nineteen-year-old kid just out of high school. Suddenly there was a large flash about 100 meters to our south, that was followed by a loud swishing sound that went right over our heads. I followed the sound and when it hit about 75 meters out there was a tremendous explosion.

I jerked three times on the cord that I was holding, and the kid sprinted back in and dove into the rice patty with us. Someone whispered loudly, "Somebody get on the radio and tell those ARVINS to stop shooting at us, we are friendlies." We had three M60 machine guns and three M79 grenade launchers in our 24-man ambush that night. After the first explosion, the M60 man on my side of the berm quickly moved to join the other M60 gunner on the side that the flash came from. Then another flash and another swish overhead and a tremendous explosion 50 meters out. Shortly after another flash and swish overhead and the explosion that happened was only 25 meters out. No one was doing anything, and I realized that they were rocket-propelled grenades and that they were walking them in on us. I figured that the next one would probably hit the patty that we were in. I whispered pretty loud to the M60 gunners on the south berm, "Somebody over there does something, the next one is going to hit us." When I said that both M60s on that side opened up, and all hell broke loose!

They had us on three sides in a crossfire. You could see green tracers going in three directions. The fire was so heavy that we were using the periscope firing position to have a chance of not being hit. The periscope position is where you stick your arm up and fire your weapon with one hand while traversing the area with fire. I heard someone whisper, they are crawling in on us. The only time that we could see anything was when ours or the enemy's muzzle flashes appeared. I thought that they might be trying to crawl in on us too, so I threw all six of my hand grenades at random areas and in different directions. Everyone else was blowing their claymores at random too because they were afraid that we would be overrun. We had heard stories of some units in our area being overrun and everyone killed, so we were doing everything that we could to not let that happen to us.

Right after I threw my last grenade there was a little slack in the firing from the enemy, so I hit my clacker three times and blew my claymore. Right after I blew my claymore, I heard a scream on the opposite side of the berm from me. I turned quickly because I thought that someone had gotten hit. I saw Sergeant Fairbanks raise and give a 20-round burst with his M16 to the area directly in front of him. At the same time, I heard Private Baumbtrong, who was in my squad, but was on the side of the patty across from me, yell, "NO, NO, that's Poatas!" At the same time, he tackled Fairbanks, but it was too late.

We were still receiving fire after that happened, so we were still firing with everything we had. One side would come under heavy fire and most of us would low crawl over to them to help suppress the fire, and then go to the next side that started receiving more fire and help them. The troops with the M79 grenade launcher laid on their backs in the middle of the rice patty that we were in and scattered rounds all around us like they were firing mortars.

During all of this action, Sergeant Cannon had gotten on the radio and called our company to tell them that we needed help. The captain told him that they were already on the way. He also called the base for gunship support. We were still firing and receiving fire, then all at once we stopped receiving incoming fire. The enemy broke and ran because they knew exactly how long it would take for gunships to get to our position and that they would be there in about five minutes.

The helicopter base that Sergeant Cannon had called for help told him that they were dispatching two Huey gunships to help us. We were in constant contact with our company and they said that they should arrive in about 12 to 15 minutes. The gunships arrived and made several passes around our position while firing rockets and M60 machine guns. They quit firing just before our company arrived, but they stayed on station until we were sure that the area was secure.

When our tracks arrived I helped put Sergeant Poatas' body in a body bag and load him onto our track. Captain Penski told us that we didn't have to stay out, so we mounted the tracks and went back to Cu Chi where we unloaded Sergeant Poatas' body at the morgue. The captain told us that there would be an investigation into Sergeant Poatas' death. Sergeant Fairbanks was all torn up because he thought that he had killed Sergeant Poatas. But later we found out from the autopsy report that AK rounds, shrapnel from the RPGs, and M16 rounds were found in his body.

Private Baumbtrong, who was in my squad, reported that Sergeant Poatas was the last one on their side to put out his claymore and that he was holding his chord for him when the RPG was fired at us. He reported that he jerked three times on the chord and that instead of running back in Sergeant Poatas started low crawling back in. Sergeant Poatas was first hit with shrapnel from the last RPG that hit close to us, and then when the enemy opened up on three sides of us, he was hit with AK rounds and then with M16 rounds. The autopsy read that he was deceased before Sergeant Fairbanks fired on him. Fairbanks had seen him in the light of muzzle flashes and had thought that he was a V. C. crawling in on us. Sergeant Poatas was a good squad leader, and we were sorry to lose him. We always had the thought go through our minds when someone was lost, "What A Waste."

Sergeant Fairbanks was also a good squad leader. I had been on many ambushes with him and had walked point for him several times. I had also been with him several times when we blew the ambushes. He was a leader that was cool and calm under fire and he knew his stuff. As the compliments went in Vietnam about a leader that was a good one. He has his crap together, which means five pounds of crap in a one-pound can. That was the best compliment that a leader could get from his men. After the inquest, he was assigned to our Charlie Company. I talked to him and he seemed to be doing fine.

The next morning Captain Penski called for me to come to his track. As soon as I got the message, I reported to him. He said, "I'm appointing you third squad, squad leader, and I'm having you promoted to specialist fourth class. So now I had the third squad of the third platoon, of Bravo Company of the 2nd 22nd Mechanized Infantry of the 25th Infantry Division, nicknamed "triple deuce" because of the 2nd-22nd.

CHAPTER 19
Lieutenant Smith Ambush

Nighttime ambushes were supposed to be illegal under the Geneva Convention, so the Army called them nighttime recon patrols, which were legal. We called them ambushes because that is what they were. We had to go on 8-man ambushes two out of every three nights. We always gripped and complained about having to go on ambushes. Lieutenant Smith, our platoon leader just couldn't understand why we hated to go on ambushes. He always said, "Man that's where most of the action is". We were saddling up and getting ready to go on ambush and he said, "I can't believe you all don't like going on ambushes." Officers didn't have to go on nighttime ambushes. We told him, "Lieutenant, why don't you get your crap and go with us?" He said, "You know, I think I will." We looked at each other and smiled when he went to get his stuff.

The tracks dropped us off 200 meters short of our ambush site. We followed standard procedures. Sergeant Cannon asked me to walk point for him again and I said, "Okay." At twilight, we moved into our ambush site and quickly set out our claymores and set up in a ditch in a bamboo hedge row. The trail we were ambushing was about 20 meters in front of us. There was quite a bit of brush grown up in the area around us. We were on 100% alert until 10:00 p.m. and it was almost 10:00 p.m. When the guy on the starlight scope said quietly, "I've got movement." Everyone got ready and we started seeing silhouettes of the enemy walking right into our kill zone. When they were about 30 meters away Sergeant Cannon blew his claymore and the rest of us blew ours immediately and opened up with our weapons.

We fired two magazines on fully auto and one on semi. The M60 gunner fired one 100-round belt and stopped. If you weren't receiving return fire that was it. We stopped, and the return fire started so we tried to build up fire superiority. After about five minutes of firing we ceased firing and we didn't receive any return fire. Lieutenant Smith had called in a Cobra Helicopter and artillery illumination. We went out to check for bodies and found five dead VC and more blood trails. The Cobra came in and fired his miniguns and rockets about 100 meters south of us when he saw enemy movement. After everything settled down we went back to our ambush position for the rest of the night. No one slept for the whole night, because there was always the chance that the enemy would regroup and ambush our ambush.

The next morning, we walked back into our logger site. Lieutenant Smith didn't say much. He never said a word to us again about gripping about going on ambushes. On every ambush, we always hoped that we didn't see anything, but this time we were kinda glad that we did.

CHAPTER 20

The Sweat Ambush

T he dry season was on and it was very hot and dry. We had to wear towels around our necks to wipe the sweat out of our eyes.

We were in an area on the north side of the Iron Triangle and we had been pulling security for the big D-12 Roam Plows that were cutting and clearing the jungle line in the area. We would guard the four big dozers in the daytime and go on ambushes at night.

After the dozers had cleared an area the helicopters would come and spray the area with agent orange to try to keep the brush from growing up. My squad leader Sergeant Sachie was taking out an 8-man ambush the first night that we were in the area and he asked me to walk point for him. I said I would because I trusted myself more than some of the other men. The area that we were supposed to ambush had brush that had grown back about head high. The area was also very flat with lots of trails and cart paths dissecting many areas of the brush. There were also many large bomb craters in the area from previous bombings.

The tracks dropped us off about 400 meters from the place where we were supposed to ambush. At about dusk, we moved out and spread out 10 meters apart. The cart path that we were on was as straight as an arrow and you could see for a long distance both up and down the path.

I was taking my time on point watching for V. C., mines, and booby trap wires. Something just told me to look behind us again and while I was stopped to look for trip wires I looked back and I saw something about 200 meters back that wasn't there before. I immediately hit the ground and so did the other seven. Sergeant Sachie crawled up to me and asked what it was. I told him that I think there are some V. C. coming from behind us. He had the scope and I told him to look through the scope if they were men that I was seeing. He looked through the scope and immediately said, "Yep! V. C.!" He motioned at the others to crawl up and when they all got there he told everyone to crawl off of the trail and then get up and move about 40 meters off of it and set up because there were some V. C. coming.

We set up a quick ambush without setting out our claymores because we didn't know if they saw us on the trail or not. We set up on the edge of a bomb crater and we didn't have much cover. The soldier beside me and I decided that we needed to do something for the cover. There were a lot of large dirt clods that had been blown out of the crater, so we quickly gathered up some and stacked them in front of us for cover. Then we set in to wait. The waiting was nerve-racking because we didn't know if they had seen us or not, and that they could be coming in behind us if they did see us. On top of the anticipation of a firefight and the heat and mosquitoes and sweat made the wait very uncomfortable. I remember continuously having to wipe the sweat out of my eyes.

We waited for about two hours, and no one showed up. We assumed that they went around us. We decided to go ahead and set up a good ambush in the same place because we were close to the trail that we were supposed to ambush anyway. We put our claymores out facing the cart path that we came in on and settled in for the night. One hundred percent alert until 10:00 p.m.

Just before 10:00 p.m., a soldier on the other end of the ambush whispered fairly loud V. C.! Everyone clicked the safety off our guns and put the claymore clacker in one hand and waited to see if we were going to blow the claymores. On ambushes, no one blew their claymore until the squad leader did. When the VC were directly in our kill zone Sergeant Sachie whispered "NOW"! and we all blew our claymores at the same time. We fired one magazine and stopped because we didn't get any return fire.

We never moved and stayed on full alert for the rest of the night. At good daylight two of us went out to check for bodies and both VC were dead from the Claymore blast. Both only had rocket-propelled grenade launchers and no AK47s. They each had four rockets. We gathered up the launchers and rockets and spread out for the walk back to the logger site.

CHAPTER 21

Sniper William Vangilder

We were working out of a firebase in the northern part of Iron Triangle, and we had been making contact with VC in the area on a fairly regular basis. We were going on a lot of Eagle Flights. About every other day the Huey helicopters would come and pick us up. There were four Hueys for every platoon and one squad would get on each helicopter. The doors were open and we would sit in the doors on both sides with our legs dangling out. There was a door gunner with a butterfly-trigger M60 machine gun on each side of the chopper. They would take us to our first objective for the day and drop us off. The helicopter pilots would always drop us off in the water if any were in the area. They would hover about six to eight feet off the ground and yell jump. You never knew how far down you would go in the mud and water. Sometimes it was up to your knees and other times up to your armpits. The reason that we would be dropped off in water was the V. C. had developed booby traps for the helicopters when they tried to land. They had rigged detonation devises with propellers that would wrap around the base when the prop blast was close enough to turn the propeller and pull the pin and set off the explosion. They had never set any of those devises in the water.

When we got our first objective and check out the area for VC or weapons, the choppers would return and pick us up. Then they would take us to the next one. This went on for most of the day. During the operations sometimes we would contact the enemy and firefights would corrupt. The firefights were with small groups of VC and most were of short duration. We usually killed two or three and the rest would break contact and sneak away. We weren't losing very many men to the firefights, but the booby traps that we were encountering were a different story. We were having troops trip booby traps about every other day that we went on Eagle flights because the area of operation that we were in was heavily booby-trapped. We had some guys killed by them, but most that tripped them were severely wounded, usually losing a leg or arm, or both.

The only one that stepped on a mackerel can booby trap that didn't go down was Big Henry. Henry was the perfect specimen of a man. He was about 6' 3" inches tall and muscular like a weightlifter. We were on a mounted patrol with the mechanized infantry tracks and we stopped to check out an area for bunkers and tunnels. Big Henry jumped off the top of their track and his foot came down right on a mackerel can booby trap. Most GIs that did that lost at least one limb, but Big Henry didn't even get knocked off of his feet. He had shrapnel wounds all over his feet, legs, and chest. We called in a dust off and they landed, and we put him on the chopper with the wounds that he had we all thought that he would be going home. But to our amazement three weeks later he came back out to join our company. Henry didn't have to fight or go on daytime patrols or nighttime ambushes anymore because he was assigned to one of our mechanic tracks.

Our sniper was short on days and the CO passed the word around asking if anyone wanted to volunteer to go to sniper school. Since none of the three snipers in our platoon ever got shot or wounded, because they didn't have to go on daytime patrols. I thought that it might be a good idea to go to sniper school and become a sniper. Maybe I would have a better chance of surviving the rest of the 365 days that I had left on my tour of duty. I went to Captain Pensky and told him that I would like to sign up for sniper school. He coyly tried to talk me out of it because I could tell that he didn't want to lose me as a squad leader. But I convinced him that I wanted to be a sniper. He said, "I'll sign you up for the next school available."

About a week later he called me to his track and told me to get on the resupply chopper that evening and that I was to attend a pre-sniper school orientation that night in Cu Chi. At the orientation, they gave us examples of what we would be able to do after completing sniper school. Some veteran snipers were there to demonstrate their skills. All the demonstrations took place after dark. They had metal targets that were from 100 meters out to 1500 meters out in the firing range. They would paint them every day with white enamel paint so that the bullet would chip out a spot so that you could look through the 50-caliber starlight scope, that was mounted on a solid tripod, and see where the rounds had hit.

The snipers were amazing. Some had M14 rifles, and some had Remington 700 30-06 caliber bolt action rifles. All the sniper rifles were fitted with a silencer and a starlight scope. We got to look through the big 50-caliber size starlight and watch where the bullets hit. I put the starlight on the 1500-meter target and watched it while two of the snipers shot at it. I would hear a click when they fired and about two seconds later you would hear a ding when the bullet hit the metal target. It was amazing, both guys hit the target almost dead center at 1500 meters.

There were ten troops there to go through the pre-sniper school. After the shooting display by the veteran snipers, they instructed us on the fundamentals of long-range shooting. I spent the rest of the night in the rear company area and the next morning I caught a chopper back to the company's logger site. The sniper school was set to start two weeks after the pre-school orientation.

Three days before I was to leave for sniper school Private William Vangilder asked if he could talk to me about sniper school. Vangilder was a member of my squad that had only been in the country for about a month. He was one of those nineteen-year-old kids that got drafted right out of high school. He was a good guy and everybody in the squad liked him. He had a beautiful girlfriend that sent him cassette tapes and provocative pictures of her about three times a week. He would show us the pictures and let us listen to the tapes. In every tape, she would always say I hope the pictures keep you guys all fired up and tell Sergeant Whalen and the rest of the squad that I'm praying for them and your safety every day.

I asked him what he wanted to talk about, and he said, "I just found out that you were signed up to go to sniper school, and I have always wanted to be a sniper." I wanted to see if I could talk you into letting me go to the sniper school because that was always my dream to be a sniper. I told him that I was already approved to go to the school, and I didn't think they would change the approval. He kept on trying to get me to let him go, so I finally told him that we would go to Captain Pensky and ask him if he could go instead of me, and if he says okay it was alright with me. We went to the captain and asked him if Vangilder could go instead of me. He said, "If it's alright with Sergeant Whalen it's alright with me." I told him that I had told Private Vangilder that if you said it was alright to change it would be alright with me. So Private Vangilder got signed up and went to Cu Chi for the two-week sniper school.

I didn't think that Captain Pensky would say that we could change, but I also knew that he didn't want to lose me as a squad leader.

After the sniper school was complete Vangilder returned to the 3rd platoon as its Sniper. I took out an eight-man ambush that night and he was my sniper. We were to ambush a trail on the west bank of a very large river, the river was about half a mile wide, and I think it was the Saigon River. It was a good night and we had good moon-light, stars, and no wind. The ambush was noneventful until right before 10:00 p.m.

The troop that had the starlight and was scanning the area with it loudly whispered, "I got movement." I immediately crawled to him and asked him, "How many and where?" He said, "Across the river and there are two of them and it looks like one has an RPG and the other an AK." I told him to give me the starlight. He handed it to me and told me where to look. I could see the RPG launcher being carried on the VC's shoulder and the other with the AK.

Private Vangilder was on the other end of the ambush and I passed the word down for him to come to me. He crawled over to me and asked, "What is it" I said, "Two V. C. on a trail across the river, you have a fire mission." He set up his gun with the bipod, ranged the distance, and locked in on his target. I was watching through the starlight when I saw the two VC stop about three seconds after they stopped I heard the action on his M14 sniper rifle work and about three seconds later I saw the lead man with the AK disappear. The other one with the RPG stepped forward and leaned over looking at where the other one went down. I don't believe that he knew what happened because the sniper rifle silencers were so good. About that time, I heard the action work again on the Vangilder rifle, and I saw the other one go down. He had his first kill as a sniper. The VC were 810 meters across the river. We returned to our logger site the next morning and after a quick breakfast of C-rations, we packed up and moved out. The captain said that we were ordered to move to a completely new area. On the way to our destination, we came upon a large area of elephant grass.

I was sitting on the left front side of the track in the squad leader's seat, which was a case of hand grenades strapped to the top of the track, and the tracking antenna was between my legs. Private Vangilder was riding on the right front side of the track with his legs over the front. The other squad members were all setting mostly close to the back of the APC. The CO had us spread our tracks out about 50 meters apart to move through the large area of elephant grass. My track was the last one on the left side of the area. I had my radio helmet on so that I could keep in contact with the CO and the other tracks. I remember looking at Private Vangilder and he smiled at me and I smiled back. About ten or fifteen meters to the left side of my track two AKs opened up and sprayed the side of my track with automatic fire. As I was turning in the direction that the fire was coming from and I saw Vangilder get hit. I flipped my safety to fully automatic and slung my M16 with one hand toward the smoke that was coming out of the elephant grass and ripped off a twenty-round burst.

Nick, my track driver, locked the left lateral and spun the track towards the fire. My 50 cal. Machine gunner pulverized the spot with a 100-round belt of ammunition and the rest of us that could fire our M16s into the tall grass. After the initial blast of fire, the V. C. didn't fire anymore. Our medic started checking on Vangilder and another soldier that took a round in his left mid-forearm. The medic told me that Vangilder took one in the side of his head and another one in his left side and that he probably died instantly. He bandaged the arm wound of the GI.

We dismounted to check out the area and we found two spider holes leading down into a tunnel system. We dropped two hand grenades into each hole hoping that the concussion might kill the V. C. I was talking to the captain on the PRICK25 radio, and I told him that we had causalities and needed a dust-off. He told me that he had already called for a dust-off and that it should be here in about 15 minutes. We set up a security circle until the helicopter arrived. When it landed in shorter grass a short distance away, we drove the track to it. We put Private Vangilder's body in a body bag and zipped it. Then we loaded him on the chopper along with the wounded man and the dust-off lifted, and we remounted our tracks. I noticed that I had a little burning pain on my right side and looked down and saw some blood on my shirt and a hole in it. I lifted my shirt and saw that I had been grazed with an AK round. The medic disinfected it and put a bandage on me.

In the chaos of the short firefight, I never noticed that the box of grenades that I was setting on took three rounds and luckily none were set off, and that the tracking antenna was shot into, and when I picked up my radio helmet I noticed that the plastic clip that you clipped to your collar was busted. The rest of my squad and I were lucky that all of us didn't get hit badly.

We drove to our new logger site and set up defenses. Captain Pensky came to my track and asked me if I wanted him to put me in for another Purple Heart. I told him "No, I already have one." I didn't know that the policy was that if you got two Purple Hearts you would be pulled from the field and given a job in the large base of the rear area. I think that may have been the reason that he picked me for the NCOIC job in the rear area during the last six weeks of my tour.

It was a big loss for us when Private Vangilder was killed. He was a joyful and friendly guy, and everybody liked him. He was just nineteen years old and got drafted right out of high school. As I thought of him, the thought in my mind was as usual… "What A Waste!"

★　　★　　★

CHAPTER 22
Sapper Attack

We had been working in the Northwest sector of the Iron Triangle Northwest of Cu Chi for about two weeks. Our company had been blowing an ambush about one out of every three nights. Most of the enemy that we were making contact with were small units of VC It was still the dry season and the mosquitos were terrible at night.

One day instead of going on a search and destroy mission in the afternoon the captain called on the radio and said we had been ordered to go west to a small fire base to pull security for it for a couple of days. We arrived at the firebase about twenty minutes before dark, so we didn't have to send out any ambushes that night.

The firebase was about an eighty-yard circle with ten tracked 155 mm artillery pieces and three 81 mm motor tracks. The 155 mm tracks were spaced all around the perimeter of the base and the motor tracks and communications tracks were located in the center of the small firebase. The area around the outside of the base was cleared for about one hundred yards out all around the base. Then there was a heavy wood line. The firebase had been established for a couple of years and there were sandbagged bunkers all around the circle and M60 machine gun fighting positions between all of the bunkers. The M60 positions were sandbagged and the guns were mounted on permanent tripods. There was a small berm and two rows of razor wire around the base.

We talked to some of the troops that were at the base and they said that they had heard that intelligence had informed their captain that the base was supposed to be attacked at any time now. The track was assigned a bunker that we could fight from and sleep in. In front of the permanent M60 fighting position was a small creek channel that ended right in front of the position and then winded out across the 100 yards of open ground to the wood line. The land had been dozed off when the base was built, but some bushes had grown back that were scattered all over the open area. The bushes were from two to four feet tall. All around the outside of the cleared area was heavily forested and jungle.

We were on alert at night just like we were when we were on an ambush. One hundred percent alert until 10:00 p.m., then one on guard with a starlight scope. The guard duty would change every two hours. Then about one hour before daylight everyone would be on one hundred percent alert. Early and late was usually when most of the enemy movement occurred.

The first night I took the first guard duty at 10:00 p.m. there was a full moon and the starlight scope was working very well because of all the light from the stars and the moon. I was scanning the area with the starlight and about fifteen minutes after I got into the M60 fighting position all of a sudden a firefight broke out about a mile east of our fire base. Someone had blown an ambush. I was listening to the radio and it was one of Charlie Company's ambushes that were in a firefight. I could see green and red tracer bullets going up in every direction. I woke everyone up so just in case we were going to be hit we would be ready.

After about fifteen minutes of the firefight, two Huey gunships arrived at the scene and started making runs firing rockets from their two rocket pods. You could see tracer bullets going to the ground from the M60 machine gunners from both sides of the gunships.

We were all in our fighting positions watching the light show, which looked like the fourth of July. It was always something awesome to see as long as you weren't in it. The two helicopters kept circling and making firing runs when all at once we could see a lot of green tracers going up to them. One of the choppers made a weird 90-degree turn and headed straight toward our position. We knew that something was not right and that they were probably hit. As the chopper got closer and closer to our fire base we could tell that it was coming down and was in bad trouble. The pilot was trying to bring it down to a friendly area. The Huey slowed down as it started to descend and the rear rotor broke and it started spinning around and around like a wasp with a broken wing. If came down with a pretty hard landing about eighty yards outside of the berm of the firebase.

We were already on our tracks to go help them when the Company Commander called on the radio and ordered the third platoon to go help them. We told him that we were already on the way. When we reached the downed chopper we got off of the tracks and formed a defensive perimeter around it. I told the track drivers and 50 cal. Gunners to stay on the tracks for security. The rest of us went to help the men in the chopper. The pilot and co-pilot were alright except for a few bruises and scraps and we got them out first. Then we checked on the M60 door gunners. One was okay, but the one on the left side of the Huey had hit hard and both of his legs were broken. The medic put blow-up splints on both legs and gave him morphine because he was in a lot of pain.

I called the captain and gave him a situation report on the injuries of the men on the shot-down Huey. He told me that he would call for a dust-off for them. We guarded the area until the dust off got there. The medics strapped the man with the broken legs to a gurney to secure his legs and put him in the chopper. The two warrant officers and the other door gunner also left on the dust off. While we were waiting for the dust off, I talked to the pilot and he said that when they got hit he had no control over where the chopper went. He said that he knew that there was a firebase in this direction, but that it was a miracle that it came straight to the firebase. He said when he saw the base in the moonlight he tried to set the Huey down as best he could.

The next morning, they sent a big Chinook track retriever helicopter out and they picked up the shot-down chopper and took it away. The second night in the firebase we didn't send out any ambushes because the Company Commander wanted us to be full force in case the base was attacked. So, we were once again on full alert with everyone in their fighting positions until 10:00 p.m. At 10:00 I had the first watch again, and I was in the M60 fighting position with the butterfly trigger M60 machine gun. It was a beautiful, bright moonlit night with no wind blowing. The starlight scope was working beautifully because of all the night light from the stars and the moon.

One thing about the night sky in Vietnam was that the stars and moon were exceptionally bright because the air was so clean. I think it was because of so little manufacturing in the country. I had been scanning the area in front of my position with the starlight for about thirty minutes. I was looking at all the scattered bushes on the cleared-off area between the wood line and the base and I almost had them memorized. All of a sudden I saw something move behind a bush. I kept the starlight on the bush until it moved again. I finally came out from behind the bush and I saw that it was a cat. It was a relief when I saw that it was a cat, not a VC.

About ten minutes later I was scanning the area again with the starlight and I found the spot where the cat had been I stopped moving the scope to see if I could find the cat again. All at once I realized that there were more bushes where the cat had been and I thought that I saw one of the bushes moving! I moved the view of the scope closer and stopped it. I counted ten more that would move about ten or twelve feet then stop then move again. I realized quickly that they were crawling in on us by pushing a bush in front of them. I quickly got on the PRICK25 radio and said, "Order 100% alert ASAP, I have movement crawling in on the north side of the base" I'm going to open up with the M60. The communications track operator said, "Roger that, notifying now."

I opened up with the M60 on the area of the bushes that I had seen moving. I shot a 100-round belt and as I was pulling the lever back to reload the M60 with another 100-round belt I looked down the ditch in front of my fighting position and I saw movement coming up the creek bed about twenty yards out. I shifted my gun to point down the ditch and gave them four 25-round bursts from my M60. About the time I was loading the third belt of ammo in the 60 everyone in every fighting position in the whole base started firing M16s, M60s, and 50caliber machine guns from the cupula of our tracks. The 82 mm mortar tracks started dropping mortars all around the base. It was like a mad minute that lasted about fifteen minutes. We couldn't figure out that night why we didn't seem to be receiving much return fire. After about fifteen minutes the cease-fire order came over the radio. We stayed on full alert for the rest of the night. We were concerned that the enemy might try to attack again.

When it got light we could see some dead Viet Cong out in front of my position. All three platoons in our Company were ordered to go out in front of our positions and check for bodies and any wounded Viet Cong. When we got to the first bodies in the ditch in front of my position we realized why we didn't receive much return fire. All of the dead VC that we found had big explosive satchel charges tied to their bodies. They had planned to crawl into the firebase and blow up the 155 mm artillery tracks and the communication tracks with their satchel charges. They didn't have any weapons other than the satchel charges on their bodies.

The Battalion Commander came out later that morning and awarded me a Bronze Star for what I did the night before. That afternoon we packed up stuff and went back to our current area of operations. Back to the two-out-of-three-night eight-man ambushes, daytime roving patrols, search and destroy missions, and Eagle flights.

CHAPTER 23
Mechanical Ambush

As our government was saying that they were winding down the Vietnam War, we knew better. They put out the news flash that they were sending the first infantry division home, but all they sent home was the top brass and the division colors back to Hawaii. They reassigned all of the troops to other units in Vietnam. We received two soldiers from the "Big Red One," as the First Infantry Division was called. Sergeant Jerry Calhoun was assigned to my platoon. I was platoon Sergeant and I assigned him to be squad leader for the second squad in my platoon, which was the 3rd platoon. He had been in Vietnam for eleven months and was a squad leader. He had extended his tour of duty for three more months so that he would be discharged from the Army when he left Vietnam. He was from Winston-Salem, North Carolina. He and I hit it off right away and became close friends. Everyone that I met from Iowa or North Carolina instantly got along with me and we became friends. I asked him why he extended his tour of duty in Vietnam when he could be almost ready to get out of there alive. He told me that he would tell me sometime.

On about the fifth day that he was in my platoon he asked me when are we going to put out any Mechanical Ambushes. I said, "What is a mechanical ambush?" He couldn't believe that we didn't set out mechanical ambushes. Sergeant Calhoun described to me how it was done. He told me that you take three claymore mines of which each had 700 steel balls in them and daisy chain them together with blasting caps on each end and then set a trip wire across the trail using spring-type clothespins. Then you run the detonation chord back to cover the full length of the detonation chord which was about 25 meters and then camouflage it. You split the electric wires apart and cut one and strip the ends and put the split wires through the back of the clothespin so that when it is closed the wires are touching. Then you take a plastic spoon out of a C-rations package break the handle off and heat the end of the trip wire and stick it through the end of the spoon handle. Wrap the wire so that it won't pull out of the spoon and then stick the spoon handle between the split wires in the clothespin. Then you go back to the end of the detonation wire and hook a PRICK25 radio batter up to it. He was very adamant that before you hook the battery up that you make sure that the kill zone is clear and that you take cover in case something went wrong and the mechanical went off unexpectedly. He said the V. C. use every kind of booby trap imaginable on us so we started using mechanical ambushes on them. He said that in the Big Red One, they were very effective. I told him, let's go talk to Captain Pensky and see what he says about setting some. Captain Pensky told us that it was probably against the Geneva Convention as unlawful warfare. Sergeant Calhoun told him that the VC and NVA use all types of booby traps against us and that they had been setting mechanicals in the Big Red One with great success. The captain kind of smiled and said, "I tell you what, I'll talk to the Battalion Commander about it and see what he says."

The next day Captain Pensky called us to his track after we had set up the logger site for the night. He said the Battalion Commander had permitted us to set out a mechanical ambush to test the results. We were both happy to hear that answer. I told the captain that I would write my wife and tell her to buy the biggest bag of spring-type clothespins that she could find and send them to me as soon as possible.

About a week later clothespins arrived. We went to the captain and told him that we have everything we need now to set out a mechanical ambush. He said, "You have the go-ahead to set out one tonight when you go on ambush."

We prepared to go on ambush with six men plus Sergeant Calhoun and myself. When the tracks dropped us off at our staging area, we quickly took cover. We told the six men to make a defensive position and wait for us to come back. When we left them we told them that we were going back up the trail that we were supposed to ambush and set the mechanical. We told them that they were not to fire at anything until we got back. We left them in the dusky light and walked side by side taking our time so that we wouldn't walk into an enemy ambush. We walked slowly with our M16s safety off and on fully automatic. Sergeant Calhoun picked a spot to set it because there was a big root wad to get behind when he hooked up the battery. I pulled security for him while he set up the mechanical. While he was doing that I had a sensation come over me that someone was watching me. I felt the hair on the back of my neck stand up. He completed setting the mechanical and we got behind the root wad to hook up the battery. After we hooked up the battery. I told him I feel like we are being watched. He said let's get out of here. We returned to the men in the same way as we went on full alert.

After we reunited with the rest of our men we quickly moved into our ambush site and set out our claymores and got ready. Just as we settled in there was a tremendous explosion from our mechanical ambush site. Calhoun was beside me and I whispered to him, "I knew that someone was watching us!" We didn't have anyone come down the trail that night, so on our way back in we went by the mechanical site and found four dead VC s and three more blood trails leaving the site. The mechanical had been effective. We gathered up the AK47s that were not destroyed and made it back to the logger site. We had successfully set the first mechanical ambush in the 25th infantry division. Shortly after that, the whole division was allowed to set mechanical ambushes.

We loggered in every night in a different spot. Standard procedure was to assign one man to set trip flairs out in front of our position one to set out claymores, two to set up the chain link rocket screen in front of the track, two to dig M60 machine gun fighting positions on each side of the track, and one to go to the middle of the circle of tracks and help dig a big hole for a garbage sump. Then we would send out three eight-man ambushes while the rest of the men would stay in for security.

When we're going to go out on a daytime search and destroy mission we would sometimes pass by some of our old logger sites. We noticed that the garbage sumps had been dug up in almost every one of them. Sergeant Calhoun and I asked Captain Penski if we could set a mechanical ambush in our current logger site garbage sump before we left the area the next morning. He permitted us to set it, we took five Bangalore torpedoes, which were seven-foot-long pipes filled with explosives, and wired them in a bundle. Then we buried them in the sump. We unscrewed the pull-firing device out of a hand grenade and screwed it at the end of one of the Bangalores.

Then we straightened out the pull-pen and tied a short piece of trip wire on it. We then took an old sock and tied the trip wire to it. The only thing left exposed on top of the garbage sump was that old sock. We also set three mechanical ambushes on three different trails leading into the clearing.

That night we loggered about a quarter mile away from our old site with the sump sock and the three mechanicals. Right before dark there was a tremendous explosion, followed by three more, whom, whoom, whoom as the three mechanicals were set off by running VC

We returned to the booby-trapped sump the next morning and there were many dead body parts and blood trails. The best that we could tell seven VC were setting around the sump when some dummy pulled on the old sock. We determined that because we found seven AK47 barrels blown about the area.

We had learned a new way to use Bangalore torpedoes other than blowing up bunkers, tunnels, and dud bombs.

CHAPTER 24

The Wolfhounds Rescue

Many times we worked in the same areas as the Wolfhounds, which was a straight-leg infantry unit of the 27th infantry division. They were very good fighters and usually kicked the behind of any enemy troops that they had firefights with, but one time one of their platoons was almost completely wiped out.

A twenty-eight-man platoon of Wolfhounds was on a night-time roving patrol about five kilometers from the Cambodian border. Shortly after dark, they walked into a long arm of an "L" shaped clearing in the jungle. They were caught in a withering crossfire from both of the outsides of the "L" shaped clearing. Before he was killed, their RTO man radioed in their position and condition. Twenty-seven men were killed and one wounded. The wounded man told us that he played dead when the NVA came out to check the bodies of the American Soldiers.

Our captain got a radio call from our battalion commander and he told him the situation with the Wolfhounds. He said that the battalion had been ordered to go in and get them out. He told him that we could be going into a major battle.

The captain called all squad leaders and platoon leaders to his track. He told us about the situation and what we had to do. He told us that it would be a Battalion size operation with Alpha, Bravo, and Charlie Company taking part in the operation.

We were about fifteen kilometers away from where the platoon had been ambushed, and Alpha and Charlie Company were about 20 kilometers away. We jumped on our tracks and headed for the Rendezvous area where we were to link up with Charlie and Alpha Companies. The road there was fairly smooth so we were able to drive the tracks to the max. The max was about 20 kilometers per hour.

We were the first company to arrive at the place where we were supposed to meet up with the other companies. The Commander had us spread out our tracks about 30 meters apart on the bamboo jungle line. While we were waiting two Bronco Spotter planes arrived on the scene and the Battalion Commander was in a helicopter circling high above us. I had my radio helmet on and could listen to all that was going on. The Battalion Commander told our captain that he had two Phantam Jets on the way with Napalm and that they should arrive in about 20 minutes.

The Battalion Commander said that Alpha and Charlie Company wouldn't arrive until about 20 minutes so he ordered us to go in. Everyone knew that we were probably in for a big fight. All the track drivers revved up their engines as loud as they could and started forward into the big bamboo and then broke them down. The sound of the diesel engines and the large bamboo popping was very loud.

We hadn't gone but about 50 meters in when the Bronco Spotter planes whose job was to mark the targets for the Phantom Jets to drop Napalm on came on the radio. I was listening and he said, "White 1, white 1, this is sunset 7 over." Our captain answered this is white 1 over. Sunset 7 was speaking with a frantic voice, do you have any friendly personnel to your immediate right front, there is a large group moving down the trail ahead of you. Our captain said, "Negative we have no personal out front of our tracks." Sunset 7 said, "My jets won't be here for 0-12 minutes all I have is white phosphorus marking missiles, with your order, I would like to give them some white phosphorus." The captain answered you have permission to fire at will. Both Bronco planes came in on dive runs and fired four missiles each. Then he came on the radio again, white 1, do you have any personal to your immediate left front? The captain answered, "That's a negative, give them some more burn!" The pilot said okay, Roger, here we come. They came in on another run and fired three missiles each. We kept busting through the bamboo and shortly after the jets arrived the Broncos fired marking rockets on targets and they dropped their Napalm bombs on two diving runs each. When the napalm exploded you could feel the air sucking from you to the site of the explosion.

After the jets left we busted into a clearing that looked bad. The captain had the tracks spread out and said for everyone to dismount and walk behind the tracks. He said for squad leaders or 50 cal. gunners and the track drivers to stay on the tracks and for the sergeants to get behind the 50 cal. I got in the 50 cal. cupula with my M16 in one hand on fully auto and my other hand on the butterfly trigger of the 50 caliber machine gun.

We immediately started finding underground bunker complexes. The troops on the ground were checking them out and throwing cook-off, hand grenades in the bunkers. A cook-off is where you let the handle pop off in your hand and count thousand one, thousand, and then stand to the side of the hole and pitch the grenade in. This doesn't give anyone inside time to pick the grenade up and throw it back out.

Before throwing a cook-off grenade in a bunker we would always say Chu Hoi which meant surrender. We approached more bunkers and I saw one facing me and I just had a feeling that someone was aiming at me. I hollered to Sergeant Calhoun, who was one of my squad leaders to check out that bunker, be careful. He stuck his M16 in the bunker hole and said Chu Hoi and someone in the bunker answered him in Vietnamese. I told my Chi Hoi scout to go to the bunker to interpret what the V. C. in the bunker said. Chu Hoi scouts were enemy soldiers that had come over to our side. Every platoon had one Chu Hhi scout. We called ours Ringo. I heard Ringo say something and then heard talk from the bunker. I asked Ringo, "What did he say," Ringo said, "he say, you kill me today, I fight you tomorrow." I told Sergeant Calhoun "Frag It!" After the frag went off Sergeant Calhoun turned and said well, he won't fight us anymore today! The next bunker also received an answer when asked to surrender. Then an AK was thrown out and a high-ranking NVA Officer came out with his hands up.

We tied his hands behind his back with zip ties and put him inside the track. He had a new 1911 Colt 45 U.S.-made semi-automatic pistol in a holster on his hip. I took the pistol from him and I carried it for the rest of the time that I was in Vietnam. We used the pistol for a tunnel gun and I carried it for a backup gun in case my M16 jammed.

We moved on through the jungle after we had checked out all of the bunkers in the complex. We came by many dead NVA that had been killed by napalm or white phosphorus rockets. We broke through the bamboo jungle and arrived at the "L" shaped clearing that the ambush had occurred in. Of the twenty-eight members of the platoon, we found one that was wounded but alive. He told us that the NVA had come out to check the U.S. bodies for weapons and to see if they were dead. He said that he survived by playing dead.

The captain called in for several dust-off helicopters to take the body bags to the morgue and to take the wounded Wolfhound to the hospital. On one chopper they also took the NVA prisoner into the base to be interrogated. The clearing that they were ambushed in was about eighty yards long and twenty-five yards wide. There were fighting positions and bunkers all along the outside edges of the "L" shape clearing. We believed that the NVA soldiers fled when they heard our tracks and the aircraft coming. The CO ordered that we spend the night in the clearing. We searched the bunkers and fighting positions and found many cases of AK rounds and 90 .82 mm mortar shells. We stacked all the mortar rounds in a hole that was made by an artillery round about ten meters behind my track. It was deep cloudy, and no moon that night and you literally couldn't see your hand in front of your face. The starlight night vision scope was useless.

When I was relieving Private Todd for guard duty at about 11:00 p.m., as I got behind the 50 caliber machine gun he said, "I thought I heard some sounds behind the track!" Later that night, another soldier said, "I kept hearing something behind the track, I think it was some kind of animal." At first, light, when everyone was on full alert and we could see, we noticed that all of the 82mm mortar rounds were gone. They had crawled in right behind my track and removed all of the mortar rounds. We figured that they had to be watching us when we stashed them there.

Shortly after the rest of the battalion arrived, which consisted of Alpha and Charlie companies. After we ate a breakfast of C-rations the Battalion Commander had all 38 tracks get on line and sweep through the area to our south. It was a mounted operation and all the soldiers rode on top of the tracks. As we swept the area we came upon numerous NVA bodies that were killed by the napalm attack. As the napalm hit them they were running down trails in large groups. Many of them melted together when they fell across each other. We were trying to find the rest of the large NVA force that had wiped out the Wolfhound platoon.

As we were going through the area we found a Huey helicopter that had been shot down. No pilots or door gunners could be found. We figured that they had walked away or had been taken, prisoner. We removed the M60 machine guns from the chopper and there was a new M16 in a rack inside the chopper. I took the M16 and used it since the one that was issued to me was an old one.

The area that we were going through changed from jungle to patches of brush and numerous small clearings. The Battalion Commander ordered us to stop and while we were stopped I looked to my right and smiled at a soldier that was on the track to my right. I had my M16 lying across my lap towards him. As we were ordered to move out we passed a clump of brush between the two tracks and just as we were clearing the brush my track hit a mackerel can booby trap on the right side of my track and the splash went toward his track. The soldier that had smiled at me was the only enlisted man in our company that had joined the Army. We had asked him why he joined and volunteered for Vietnam he said, "I just wanted to see what combat was like." The track stopped again, and I looked at him and saw blood on his left shoulder I asked him, are you hit? He gave me a weird look and said, "Sergeant Whalen you shot me." I said, "I didn't shoot you, we hit a booby trap." He thought because my M16 was pointed in his direction that it had gone off and hit him. All of a sudden he passed out and fell off the track. We rushed to him to check him out we thought that the shrapnel from the booby trap went through his arm and into his chest cavity. I looked at his arm and I could see a sliver of metal sticking out of his arm. I reached down and pulled it out. It had penetrated only about ¼ of an inch. He then came too and said again, why did you shoot me? I said I didn't shoot you here is what hit you. He had just fainted when he saw blood on his shoulder.

We never did locate or make contact with the NVA that had ambushed the Wolfhound platoon, but the Air Force Bronco Spotter planes and the Phantom Jets with napalm killed a large number of them. When we finished sweeping the area all three mechanized infantry companies were ordered by the Battalion Commander to return to their area of operations.

CHAPTER 25
Minefield

We were working in an area west of Cu Chi about twelve miles from the Cambodian border. The area had a heavy jungle with some cart paths going through it. Our mechanized company was going through the jungle area on a cart path. My platoon had point and my track was second in line and the rest of the company tracks were spaced out behind us. We had gone about 400 meters down the path when the track in front of us hit a mine. The shock wave almost knocked us off of our track and it sent all of the men on the track airborne unqualified as we called it. The soldier in the 50-caliber hatch was the only one that got hurt. His injury was very painful and serious. The whole 50 caliber cupula gun and all was blown off with him in it and it came down on his femur and both legs were severely broken. The CO called a dust-off for him. Two medics put blow-up splints on his legs and gave him morphine to keep him as comfortable as they could until the dust off got there. We dismounted the tracks and set up a defensive perimeter until the helicopter left with the injured man. There was no place for the dust off to land in the heavy jungle so they hovered in place and cabled down a basket. The medics secured him on the basket and they winched him up through the trees and away they went.

As soon as the chopper left the captain called me on the horn and said, "Sergeant Whalen, you and Sergeant Winborn take the mine detector and clear the path ahead." I told him, Yes Sir, on our way. Winborn and I told our guys don't shoot ahead because we are going to be out there. While we were getting the mine detector ready, the second squad started the repair work on their track. The damage could be fixed by the squad. The mine blew one idler wheel off and broke the track. We always carried extra idler wheels and pieces of track so that we could fix the tracks if the damage was like this.

Sergeant Winborn and I started sweeping the trail with the minesweeper. We walked side by side and kind of back to back to be ready for anything. We both had our M16s safety off on fully automatic. He run the mine sweeper while I scanned the surroundings for anything out of the ordinary. I carried the PRICK25 radio on my back.

We didn't find anything for the first 100 meters. The captain called me and asked how far we had gone. I told him that the first 100 meters is clear. He told us to come back to the tracks so we started slowly working our way back. The squad on the damaged track was taking longer than the captain thought it should take to repair it. He got impatient and ordered my track driver to go around the damaged track. When he got about 20 meters passed the damaged track, he hit a mine. The explosion sent my guys on top in the air and when they came down, no one seemed to be injured except for eardrums and bruises. The mine did the same damage to my track as the other one, one idler wheel and a broken track.

The captain called me on the radio and said, "I thought you said you and Winborn couldn't find any more mines!" I answered we have had no readings at all sir. We kept slowly working our way back to the tracks. I was scanning the ground and I saw a little something sticking out of the ground that didn't look right. Sergeant Winborn's footprint was right on it. I got down for a closer look and I told Winborn it looks like a piece of green plastic. I took out my wooden probing knife and started removing dirt from around the object. It was a mine. Sergeant Winborn had stepped right on it when we were sweeping the trail. Luckily the firing device was set so that a man couldn't set it off, just a track or tank. When we got the mine completely dug up we could see that it was completely made out of fiberglass and a mine sweeper couldn't pick it up. I called the CO and told him that we had found a solid fiberglass mine and that was why we didn't find the one that my track had hit.

In about an hour, we had both tracks repaired enough to move out. We were ordered to bust through the jungle and stay off of the cart path. Since my track had moved around the point track we moved out with my track on point. It was hard busting through the thick jungle and the going was slow. Our tracks were making a lot of noise as the drivers had to reeve up the engines to bust over some of the vines and trees. Lieutenant Smith had been riding on the point track so when mine took point he mounted mine. He was doing the navigation for us.

After we had traveled about 400 meters we come up to an "L" shaped clearing. Lieutenant Smith told my track driver to go straight ahead which would be right in the kill zone of the "L" shaped clearing. If the V. C. had an ambush set up for us, we would all be dead. We told him, Sir, this is stupid. If a place looks bad, and this one does, you go around it, not right through the kill zone! We talked him into going around the outside of the clearing. As we were in the jungle but close to the outside edge of the clearing we could see freshly dug fighting positions in the hedgerow of bamboo that lined the edge of the field.

We stopped in our tracks and dismounted to check the area out. We found tunnels and spider holes all along the edge of the clearing in the hedgerows. Lieutenant Smith called the CO and told him what we had found. He told us to blow the tunnels and spider holes up with Bangalore torpedoes. We screwed a bunch of Bangalore's together all along the tunnel system and put a 3-foot-long burn fuse on the last one. The captain told us to light the fuse and for all four 3rd platoon tracks to quickly move away by about 100 meters from the end of the explosives, and that the rest of the company should stay where they were. We lit the fuse and quickly moved out about 100 meters. Shortly after we stopped there was a tremendous explosion that shook us with us over 100 meters away. We didn't have time to check for bodies or anything because it was getting late in the afternoon and we needed to get to a secure clearing to set up a logger for the night.

CHAPTER 26

Big Operation Before Cambodia

Immediately after we found the shot-down Huey helicopter and stripped it of the weapons and ammo that were left in it, we mounted back up on our tracks. I kept the brand-new M16 that was strapped inside the chopper and used it the rest of the time that I was in the field. The Wolfhound recovery operation was complete. The captain stopped his track and told us on the radio that we were ordered to make a fast trip to Cu Chi and to get there as soon as possible.

When we arrived in Cu Chi he called a meeting of all squad leaders, platoon sergeants, and platoon leaders. He told us to triple all ammunition and C-rations, and that we would be going on a major operation. Also that the operation would be a battalion size operation.

We all got busy loading more ammunition and C-rations on the tracks. We always carried lots of ammunition on the tracks anyway that was a good thing about mechanized infantry. You didn't have to worry about running out of ammo. But we loaded all we could get in the track anyway. This was the night that President Nixon was supposed to give an important speech and we all hoped that he was going to pull us out and send us home.

By the time Nixon was to give his speech, we had finished loading the tracks and everyone was grouped up around radios to listen to it. I'll never forget when he made the statement, "The U.S. forces have not and will not step foot on Cambodian soil." We all looked at each other silently, and then in unison we all said, "We're going to F'n Cambodia!"

CHAPTER 27
Pre-Invasion

After spending the night in Cu Chi and tripling our ammo and provisions we left for the Cambodian border. We traveled on a two-lane paved highway that some guy said was Highway One. It was the only paved road that we had been on since I arrived in Vietnam. Because the road was smooth, we could drive our tracks at maximum speed which was around thirty-five miles an hour. Along the way, we had to watch for any disturbance on the surface of the paved road to prevent us from hitting any mines that may have been planted in the road.

As we traveled along toward the border we got to see a lot of different people doing the things the Vietnamese people had probably done for centuries. Farmers were out in their rice patties plowing with a wooden plow pulled by their water buffalo. Women were repairing rice patties and some were planting rice sets in the rice patties that were flooded. The impression that you got of the people out in the countryside was that they just wanted to be left alone by both sides in the war.

About 10:00 a.m. we arrived at the staging area for the invasion. I had never seen so many troops and equipment and weapons. It made me think of what the preparation for an attack in WWII must have looked like.

The engineers were just about to complete an instant airstrip. Air Force bombers had come in the night before and dropped giant bombs that exploded just before they hit the ground and completely blew all of the trees and debris out of an area that was about ¼ mile wide and ¾ long. Then Chinook Helicopters brought in Bulldozers to level the land and build a berm around the area. Then many Chinooks brought in big loads of P.S.P. which were sheets of pierced steel planking that locked together to make what we called instant airstrips and helicopter landing pads.

When we arrived the engineers were just completing putting down all of the P.S.P. for a huge airstrip. Cargo planes were already landing on part of the strip and all kinds of helicopters were in the air and on the ground everywhere. There were several companies of tracked artillery, mostly 155mm, settled in all around the berm with many units of infantry both straight leg and mechanized filling in gaps all around the big instant base. Along with the Phantom Jets, and helicopters, flying all around. B-25 Bombers flying over so high that you could barely see them. The whole spectacle was an awesome sight to see. The B-52s were already dropping bombs about 10 miles from us inside Cambodia. They were prepping the area for our invasion. Even from 10 miles away when the bombs from the B-52s started exploding we could feel the ground shake.

As the day went on more and more battalions of troops were arriving in the staging area. We knew that we were close to a river that divided Vietnam from Cambodia in the area that we were in and that we would have to cross it somehow. We didn't know that the combat engineers were going to go in that night to construct a pontoon bridge across the river but they did. The area that we were going to cross into was known as the Dogface area because the bends on the river in that area made the shape of a dog's face on the map.

That night our new captain volunteered my 3rd platoon to go on a mounted ambush on a straight dirt road south of the big new base. We were to stay on our tracks and if we got hit or initiated contact with the enemy we were to return fire and come back into the base as soon as possible.

We arrived at our ambush spot right before dark. The platoon sergeant told us squad leaders to keep everyone at full alert all night. We were about three-quarters of a mile from the base. He also told us to keep the Track drivers ready to fire up the engines at the first sign of anything.

That night was one of the very dark nights that we sometimes experienced in Vietnam. It was deeply cloudy and you actually couldn't see your hand in front of your face. Needless to say, we were all very scared because we knew that there were numerous NVA units in the area. About an hour after dark, we thought that we heard some sound from the wood line. On each side of the road that we were on, it was about fifty meters to the wood lines.

All at once, in the dead quiet night, RPGs were fired at us from both sides of the road and then we started receiving automatic AK fire. Both RPGs missed the tracks and we could see the green tracers of the AKs going over our heads. Everyone started firing everything that we had at the wood lines on both sides of the road. The track driver immediately fired up the tracks and took off at full throttle. We kept firing all the way back into the new base. I had my squad leader's helmet on and I heard the captain calling for an artillery strike on the area that we had just left. Then he asked the platoon sergeant if he had any casualties and he answered, "Don't think so sir." I believe the V. C. missed us because it was so dark that they couldn't see us any better than we could see them. The officers believed that what we experienced was just a probe.

The artillery pulverized the area that we had just come from with 155mm rounds. We were afraid that we would have to go back out, but we didn't. We spent the rest of the night in the new base which was called Tan Uyen Airstrip.

★ ★ ★

CHAPTER 28

Invasion of Cambodia

O n the day of the invasion of Cambodia, we staged forces about a mile from the border. The engineers had gone in the night before and constructed a pontoon bridge across a small river that designated the border. We were to cross the bridge and enter Cambodia in what was known as the Dogface region. All of the operations that day were to be battalion size. Our Battalion Commander told Bravo company to take the lead and the Company Commander ordered the 3rd platoon, my platoon to take point, and my track would be the first one in. We were all very sober and I think that we all expected to die that day.

While we were stopped we were told that B-52 bombers were almost there and that we couldn't get any closer to the drop zone until the bombing was over. Once the bombs started exploding the whole ground was shaking from the concussion of the 500-pound munition going off.

Once the bombing stopped the CO ordered me to advance with caution. We were the first track to cross. There was a cart path to drive on and immediately we started seeing half-dug fighting positions on both sides of the trail with the little entrenching shovels thrown down where they had dropped them and ran.

Crossing into Cambodia was like entering a new world. The terrain, jungle, houses, and everything was different. It was a beautiful land. After traveling down the cart path for about one-half mile, we came to a crossroad, and as we moved up where we spotted two NVA soldiers sitting on a double bicycle with SKS rifles strapped across their backs. They were looking back at us with a shocked look on their faces. When they started to get their rifles off of their backs Private Baumbtrong, who was settling on the left front of my track, gave them a twenty-round burst from his M16. Both were killed instantly. Baumbtrong jumped off of the track to check them out and I told him to get their weapons and ammo belts. The captain called me on the horn and asked what happened. I told him that we had killed two NVA that were on a double bicycle. He said, "What!" I told him, you heard it right, on a double bicycle. He ordered me to keep advancing.

After about another four hundred meters we broke into a large clearing that was about four hundred meters long and one hundred meters wide. The CO told me to enter the clearing and hold the position while the rest of the company tracks spread out to my left and right. There were several houses inside the edge of the wood line on the opposite side of the clearing straight in front of my track. When all twenty tracks were about to complete getting in their positions, we saw an NVA officer in full-dress uniform start running from one house to another. Private Penski, who was my third squad grenade launcher man just threw up and launched one M79 round at the NVA officer. He hit close to him, but he kept running. The CO immediately came on the radio and yelled, "Who fired that round" I told him my track did sir, we saw an NVA officer running away. He said, "No more firing unless I give the order."

As we were about ready to advance, about forty old Cambodian men came walking out of the wood line in front of my track. They all had gingham loin cloths and sashes on and all of their hands were up. All of the gingham dress was the same color. They started walking straight to my track and when they got close I could see a grave look on their faces. We all had the safeties off on our weapons because we didn't know what to expect. When they got directly in front of my track they put their hands together and started bowing repeatedly to us. Ringo, my Chu Hoi scout was sitting beside me. I asked him, "Can you speak Cambodian," He said, "Yes," I asked him to jump down and see what they want. He jumped off the track and walked up to the one that looked like the leader. Ringo spoke with him for a while, and then he turned toward me. I said, "What did he say Ringo" Ringo said, "he says NVA says American soldiers come and they kill all men and rape all women," He said that they came as a sacrifice to prevent us from doing that. I told Ringo, you tell him we are not going to kill any of their men or rape any of their women, and that we are here to help. We are only here to kill NVA. Ringo returned to them and told them what I said and a big smile came on all of their faces and you could see the relief on their faces. They put their hands together and above their heads and started bowing to us in thanks. After the old men left, the CO asked me what they wanted. I told him what they said about the NVA and what I told them. He then told everyone to get ready to advance.

After the captain gave the order to move out we started moving across the clearing toward the houses. We were spread out in about a two-hundred-yard line. We had just started moving when all of a sudden the right side of our formation started receiving fire from the wood line behind us. We all spun our tracks around and the captain gave the order to open fire with all you got. We pulverized the wood line with 50-cal and M60 machine guns, M16s fire, and grenade launchers. We fired for about two minutes, and we stopped receiving fire. Luckily no one was hit.

After we stopped receiving fire we turned back and moved across the clearing past the houses. As we went through the only peo-ple that we saw were old men and young boys. We traveled through the jungle in a single file with my trackback on point. We had gone about another 500 meters when we broke into another clearing and we could see some bomb damage around some of the houses. I had my track stop while I annualized the situation. We saw a young Cambodian man carrying a baby start walking toward us. All he had on was a loin cloth so I knew that he probably wasn't a threat. When he got close I could see that he had tears in his eyes and that the baby boy, which looked like he was about ten months old, had a large wound on his left thigh. I told Ringo to jump down and talk to him. Ringo talked to him and then told me that he said bombs hit his house last night and that his wife was killed and his baby was hurt. Everyone on the track agreed that we should call in a dust-off to take the baby to the hospital. I got on the radio and told the Company Commander the situation and he said, "Forget it, we don't have time to mess with these people." I had my medic Doc Adams jump down and dress the baby's wound. He did the best that he could do with antibiotics and bandages. Then the CO told me to move on out. All the guys in my squad were angry that the CO wouldn't let us take care of the baby. We started to realize that our new captain was lacking in humanity.

NCOIC Sergeant Michael Whalen with his good buddy Sergeant Jerry Calhoun on the right just before he went home.

My track driver Private Rich Nicol "Nick" at Tan Uyen air strip after 46 days of combat in Cambodia.

Sergeant Whalen in front of his track after it got hit by a rocket propelled grenade that came through the rocket screen during the skull fire fight.

This is my third squad track after we hit a mine and went "air borne unqualified."

Sergeant Whalen in the M-60 fighting position in the
fire base where he helped repel a sapper attack.

Some members of my platoon that I was getting ready to go on an
ambush with. Back row, left to right: Private Rich Nicol, Private
Al Nazario and Private Dave Linsey. Front row, left to right:
Private Jalen Brown, and third platoon Staff Sergeant Rut Laff.

Private Andy Andrety on the left, Ringo our Chu Hoi Scout center and Sergeant Michael Whalen at the second night logger site in Cambodia.

Sergeant Michael Whalen when he was a private getting ready to go on ambush.

Private Rich Pewshinski showing off with some
other squad members by my track.

I was setting on the ammo cans on top of the track when the
piece of shrapnel I'm pointing at hit right below me.

A member of my platoon, Private Dan Lake at Tan Uyen
right after we returned to Vietnam from Cambodia.

Private Marshal Tucker, on the left, and platoon leader Lieutenant
Smith at the airstrip after returning from Cambodia.

141

My company's tracks lined up to go on a day
time search and destroy mission.

The Cambodian man who gave us showers and supper. Left to right,
Private Andy Andrety, Private John Bauntrong, Sergeant Michael Whalen,
the Cambodian man and three of his children, and Specialist John Brown.

Members of my platoon who became hardened combat soldiers at Ten Uyen Air Strip after 46 days in Cambodia. Left to Right: Private William Vangilder, Private Rich Nickle, Private Gary Todd, Sergeant Dailey, and Private Marshal Tucker.

Soldiers just back from 46 days in Cambodia. Left to Right: Private Steve Harken, Private Earl Raby, Private Lee Hart, Private Marshal Tucker, and Private Gary Todd.

Lieutenant Smith 3rd Platoon Leader at Tan Uyen after Cambodia.

Private Earl Raby from Arkansas at Tan Uyen Air
Strip after the invasion of Cambodia.

Private Gary Todd at Tan Uyen after surviving 46 days in Cambodia.

The ARVN soldier with his pet snake.

Bravo Company First Sergeant Tinga in headquarters at Cu Chi.

★ ★ ★

CHAPTER 29

First Night in Cambodia
The Bait

On our first night in Cambodia, our new Company Commander volunteered Bravo Company to set up a logger site about a mile from the battalion logger site. We were to be used as bait to try to get the NVA to attack so that the rest of the battalion could come to our rescue.

We set up a logger site in about a four-acre clearing and set out two rows of claymore mines, two rows of trip flairs, and rocket screens in front of each track. We dug a fighting position on each side of the track and dug one in front of each track and then pulled the track over it. The reason for that was that we were pretty sure that if we were attacked there would be a mortar barrage before the main attack. If you have ever been under mortar attack you would understand the terror that you feel. You can hear the round hit the bottom of the tube and pop then sizzle up and then you can hear it sizzling, coming down and you don't know where it is going to hit. Pure terror for everyone! We dug the fighting position for us to get in under the track so that we could have some overhead cover in case of a mortar attack.

We had permission to have as many mad minutes as the CO wanted. When it was almost dark he called on the radio and said,

"Mad minute in 0-1 minute." We fired our M16s, M60 machine guns, and 50-cal machine guns as many rounds as we could in one minute. We pretty well devastated the jungle wood line around us.

About 45 minutes later we had another mad minute. The purpose of the mad minute was supposed to deter the enemy from mounting an attack on us. But, this time we thought it was probably done so that the enemy could find us and attack us.

We were preparing for a third mad minute when all hell broke loose. But, the plan didn't work, they didn't attack us, they attacked the battalion logger site. We could hear all the firing and see tracer rounds going in every direction, both red and green. Green was the enemy. I had my radio helmet on and I listened to the Commander ask the Battalion Commander if he wanted us to come and help and he said, "Negative, hold your position." A few minutes later the Cobra Gunships arrived on the scene and the fireworks exploded. Their mini guns and rockets and automatic grenade launchers always looked like the 4th of July. By the time the Cobras got to the battalion position they had stopped receiving fire, but the Cobra Choppers fired their guns and rockets on all trails that they could see with their inferred night vision helmets. We just knew that we would get hit sometime during the night, so we were on full alert all night.

When daylight came and we were not hit we still knew that we were in extreme danger of being ambushed. The Battalion Commander called and ordered us to break the logger site and come and rejoin the rest of the battalion. We told each other, one day, one night, and we are still alive. We broke the logger site and returned to the big clearing where the rest of the battalion was set up in. I inquired about casualties from Charlie company, one soldier told me that one man had been killed and three wounded when an RPG hit a fighting position.

When we rejoined the battalion we spent the rest of the day with our tracks online sweeping the countryside looking for NVA.

★　★　★

CHAPTER 30

Second Night in Cambodia
Ambush Alley

O n our second night in Cambodia, the battalion loggered into another large clearing. There were about eight or ten Bamboo Houses just inside the tree line. Our track was right in front of one. The Cambodian man that owned the house came up to me by our track and smiled and said something to me. Ringo our Chu Choi scout was two tracks back and I yelled for him to come to my track. Ringo could speak Vietnamese and Cambodian. I asked Ringo to interpret for me. I said, "See what he wants" Ringo talked to him for a while, and then he told me that the Cambodian man said he was glad to see the U.S. soldiers because the NVA treated them badly and that he invited me and my squad to bathe at his well and have supper with him and his family.

I liked all of the Cambodian people that I met while we were in Cambodia. They were good hard working honest people. As we drove our tracks down the cart paths Cambodians would come out and toss pineapples up to us. Stalk-ripened pineapples were the best pineapples I'd ever eaten. I practically lived on them for the first two weeks in Cambodia. Sometimes we would pitch a can of C-rations to them if they gave us a pineapple.

Most of the houses we saw in Cambodia were all bamboo and thatch. They were all on stilts because of rain in the rainy season. Everything in their houses was made from bamboo or thatch or wood. The only manufactured things I saw in their houses were their clothes. They wore gingham loin cloths and skirts, and the small children never wore clothes. In different areas of Cambodia, you would see a different color of gingham. Everyone in the area wore the same color of gingham. It must have been a tribal thing.

The Cambodian man led us to his well and he cranked up water from his hand-dug well and poured it over us as we stripped our clothes off and soaped up. Then he rinsed us each off with a bucket of water over our heads. After the shower, we put our clothes back on and he told Ringo to tell us that supper was ready and that he would be honored to have us as guests. We entered his home and his wife and kids welcomed us and led each of us to a bamboo chair around a large bamboo table. The meal was very good as most of the food was fruit, bananas, mangos, pineapples, some rice and peanut mix, and some kind of fruit juice. We enjoyed the meal and his family was very friendly to us. We thanked him for his hospitality and returned to our track.

I heard the radio on the track squawk so I jumped up on it and put the radio helmet on and listened to the conservation between our company commander and the battalion commander. The battalion commander told him that the 10-kilometer stretch of road between the river and our position was bad and that every supply convoy that tried to come through that day had been ambushed and turned back. I listened as our company commander volunteered Bravo Company to run the road at night and try to draw fire. The Battalion Commander said, "I'll give you the job, but I want you to recon by fire the whole length of the road." As soon as they signed off the CO called all squad leaders, platoon sergeants, and platoon leaders to his track. For once we were told what the mission was, and everyone that had tried to come down that road today had been ambushed. He said to get your men coordinated so that when your tracks are ordered to fire that one machine gun shoots to the left side and the other to the right. Once we start moving we moved fast and keep a continuous fire to the river through "ambush alley."

I got my platoon members together and quickly explained to them what we would be doing and that they get a buddy team member to take turns loading and shooting the machine guns, and changing out barrels if needed. Get everything together so that you can get what you need quickly. Let's show the NVA what Mechanized Infantry can do!

I was behind the cupula 50-cal and we had another 50-cal without a shield mounted on the left rear side of my track and an M60 Butterfly machine gun on the right rear side. I told the other 50 gunners that he and I should take turns firing to try to keep our barrels from overheating while I was firing he could be reloading and while he was firing I would be reloading. That way we could keep up a continuous rate of fire.

Ambush Alley was a straight flat road with forest and jungle on both sides of the road. We were told that all the units that got ambushed on the road were hit with rocket-propelled grenades and 51-caliber machine gun fire. When we arrived at the straight stretch of the road the Company Commander told us to space out about 25 meters apart and to start recon by fire when the first track started moving out. The track drivers laid the hammer down on the throttles and we were moving about as fast as the tracks could go while laying down a tremendous base of fire. You could see tracer bullets ricochet off of trees and the ground. You could see 50-cal machine gun tracer bullets go in one side of a two-foot-thick mahogany tree and pop out the other side and keep going.

It probably took us about twenty-five to thirty minutes to run the length of the road to the river. We fired many hundreds of rounds on the way. Although my squad member and I were firing the 50-cal machine guns and were getting a break while the other one was firing the guns got hot. The 50-cal barrels got cherry red hot and I could see the rifling in the barrel when I fired it. About the time we finished our run, we were starting to get cook-off rounds, which meant that the shells were exploding before they were completely in the chamber because of the heat. That is a dangerous situation when you start getting cook-off rounds as part of the hull will blow out the side of the gun. Just as I told the other 50-gunner that we were going to have to let our barrels cool we reached the river and everyone stopped firing anyway. Our M60 machine gun didn't get too hot because we had two extra barrels for it and the two-man crew had changed out both barrels along the way.

We stayed by the river for about thirty minutes to let all of the guns cool down, and then the CO informed us over the radio that we were going back down the road and to be ready to fire if we start receiving fire, but save your ammo if we don't get hit. We were ready for anything on the trip back through Ambush Alley, but we never received any fire back.

The only causality that we had was a soldier on the third track from the front that got hit in the ankle somehow by a ricocheted round somehow bounced off of something and came back and hit him in the ankle.

The next day several convoys came down Ambush Alley Road and no one got ambushed. So, I guess our firing run down the road must have done quite a bit of damage to the enemy. All the time that we were in that area after the run no one got ambushed going down Ambush Alley Road.

★ ★ ★

CHAPTER 31

Leaving Cambodia
Lightening Combat
Leaders Course LCLC

On my sixth day in Cambodia, it was time for me to go to Cu Chi for the five-day Lightening Combat Leaders Course. The 25th Division sent a Loach helicopter to pick me up. The pilot was a nice guy, like most helicopter pilots, he asked me to sit up front with him in the co-pilot seat. We lifted off from the logger site and he gained altitude as fast as he could. We got up as high as I had seen helicopters fly. He said, "It's pretty safe for choppers at this altitude."

We marveled at how pretty the Cambodian countryside was from up high. Although we knew that on the ground it was a different story. The pilot asked me if I had ever flown a helicopter before. I told him no, he said it's not hard. Just a few things to learn, he said this handstick does this and the other one does this, as he demonstrated what the moves caused the chopper to do. Then he said, put your feet on both floor pedals and when my feet were on the pedals he moved them to show me what they were used for. He said, keep your hands on the sticks and your feet on the floor pedals and move them as I move them to get the feel of it. As he did the maneuvers, I was moving the controls with him and he made it look easy. We turned to the left and the right and up and down. He said, "Okay here you go, take it awhile."

I started correcting our direction and altitude. Every move that I made was an overcorrection! He hadn't been moving all the controls as much as I thought. The chopper looked like a wasp with a broken wing, going up and down and half around. He was dying laughing at me. I think he knew what would happen when I took control. After a while, I kinda got it halfway under control and he took the controls. He told me, not too bad for the first time. I thought that it was pretty bad. Also, I thought, man if something happens to him I'll be in real trouble.

We crossed back into South Vietnam and before long he dropped me off on a chopper pad not far from my company area. Before I got off of the chopper the pilot shook my hand and said, good luck man, you are a good sport. I thanked him for the experience and jumped off of the chopper and headed for the company area.

★ ★ ★

CHAPTER 32
LCLC

My squad leader, Sergeant Poatas was killed. When our ambush got ambushed Captain Penski made me squad leader of the 3rd squad, 3rd platoon. He also had me promoted to Specialist fourth class. The next day the captain picked me for another assignment.

Every month the second of the twenty-second held a five-day in-country leadership course and every company in the battalion sent one man each time to the class. Captain Penski picked me to attend the next class which was to begin in three weeks. The class was to be held in our home base at Cu Chi. Little did I know that I would be in Cambodia when the class was to be held. The day before we. were to leave for the Cambodian border, Captain Penski got his six months in the field complete and we got a new company commander.

The name of the course that I was to attend was Lightening Combat Leadership Course, or as the grunts called it LCLC. The course was a refresher class in navigation by compass, mine, and booby trap detection, conducting ambushes, calling in artillery and mortar fire, calling in helicopter gunships, (Cobras and Hueys) weapons refresher course, calling in Phantom Jets, demolition with C-4 explosives, and leadership skills. There were eighty men in the class from all over the 25th Infantry Division. They told us that at the end of the training, we would be given a test and that whoever scored the highest would automatically be promoted a rank. I didn't think much about that but, I did think now I am in charge of my squad members and their lives will depend a lot on what I do or don't do. I decided that I didn't want to get someone killed because of a mistake that I made. So, during all of the training, I took notes like it was a college class and studied them every night. I wanted to know all of the stuff forwards and backward. They also told us that the man that scored the highest on the test would also get to take out an 80-man ambush for the final night of training.

When they gave the hundred-question test and scored it, they announced my name and said that I was the only one to make a perfect score. I was to get promoted in a ceremony to Sergeant E-5, and then I would be taking out the 80-man ambush. That afternoon they had the service and they presented me with my stripes. Two Staff Sergeants put the stripes on each shoulder and gave them a hand-fist hit at the same time. That ended the ceremony. They then told us that it was time to start mounting up for the 80-man ambush.

The officer in charge told me that I would have the best point dog and his trainer to walk point for me and that one of his top snipers would also go. He gave me the coordinates of the ambush site and all the call signs of the artillery, gunships, and mortars in the area. We grouped up inside the fence and I picked a man to be my radio man (RTO). I had six troops with M60 machine guns, six with M79 grenade launchers, and the rest had M16s.

We left the compound and had about fifteen hundred meters to go to get to our ambush site. All of the men walked ten meters apart so that one burst of AK or machine gun fire could not get a bunch of people at a time. We were strung out about half a mile long. The dog man was out front, then the guy I picked to walk point, then me and my RTO, then the sniper, and the rest of the 80 men. We hadn't gone far and the dog alerted, I moved up to the handler and I asked him, what is it. He said it was his buried metal alert. The dog was looking at one spot on the ground and would not look away. Then the handler took a wooden probe and dug with it. At about six inches deep he found a small piece of barbed wire. The dog was very good! He didn't miss anything. When we got within about 300 meters of our ambush site we came out into an open area about five hundred meters square. The dog alerted and everyone dropped to the ground. I low crawled up to the dog handler and asked him what had he been alerted to, and he answered it was his small unit alert. About that time we saw the VC come out from hiding and started walking fast toward the far side of the wood line. I motioned for the sniper to come forward. When he crawled up I pointed at the VC and he started setting up the bipod on his sniper rifle. He was the only sniper that I saw in Vietnam with an M16 for a sniper rifle.

The VC was about 250 meters out when he fired his first shot. Dust flew behind the V. C. and he started running. The sniper shot at him three more times and after every shot the VC would catch a new gear in speed. He made it to the wood line and got away. We moved on into the middle of the big clearing and found the trail that we were supposed to ambush. I found a good-sized rice patty with dikes that were about two and one-half feet high. I had everyone set up the ambush on the south, west, and east sides of the rice patty. I deployed two M60 machine guns on each of the sides of the ambush. Six M79 grenade launchers were deployed the same as the machine guns, and all the rest of the ambush members had M16s.

We completed our setup and went to one hundred percent alert. About thirty minutes after dark I was in the middle of the south side and the troops down at the end of the line on my right where the dog was passed the word to me that the dog handler wanted to see me. I low crawled down to him and as I got close the dog was between me and him and he started growling at me. I said he won't bite me, will he? The handler answered, no. So, I crawled on by the dog and he bit me on the back of my thigh! I said he bit me! He said he has never done that before, and he gave the dog a whispered scolding. After the scolding, the dog went back on alert. He was looking to our south and was emitting a continuous low growl. I asked the handler what that meant. He answered, "That is his medium size unit alert." Then we saw two flashlights come on just inside the wood line that the dog was alerting to. I got on the radio and called the artillery station and told them that I had a fire mission for the 155s. I gave them my estimated coordinates.

I estimated the distance at four hundred meters to our Southeast. I stayed on the radio with the artillery officer and he informed me the round is ready. They always only fired one round first in case you were not accurate in your coordinates. As the artillery units fire a round, they say "hang it" on the radio to let you know that the round is on the way. You tell everyone to get down and just before the round hits they will say "splash." The first round hit right on the flashlights and of course, they went out. I told the artillery officer, on target, on target, fire for effect. They fired about twenty 155MM explosive rounds into the area. We did not have any more alerts or see anything for the rest of the night.

The next morning, we walked back to Cu Chi. Our column was strung out again for about a half mile with eighty men walking ten meters apart. When we got to Cu Chi everyone said goodbye and headed off to catch a helicopter back to where their company was. I took a chopper back to Tan-Uyen airstrip and then a resupply chopper back to my company in Cambodia.

CHAPTER 33

The Bridge in Cambodia
My First Mission as Platoon Sergeant

When I returned to my company in Cambodia after getting my sergeant stripes at LCLC the captain called me to his track and told me that Sergeant Campbell and Specialist Rasmussen had been in an ambush two nights ago and both had been killed. Sergeant Campbell was the platoon sergeant for the 3rd platoon. The CO told me that he was assigning me as the third platoon sergeant.

For the first few days in Cambodia, we went on search-and-destroy missions during the day and set up a defensive logger site every night. Some nights we would send out ambushes.

On the afternoon of my third day back the captain called me to his track. He told me that the intelligence was that the NVA was going to blow up a main resupply bridge across a small river that was about three kilometers to our east. He said that the bridge was crucial for us because it was a long way up and down the river to other bridges.

He told me, "I want you to take your platoon there and secure the bridge for the night." He said, "Take all four infantry tracks and I will give you two mortar tracks and you have permission to have as many mad minutes as you want." A mad minute is when everyone opens up with all weapons that they have for one minute. You never wanted to set a schedule so you have them at random times to confuse the enemy and maybe keep them from attacking. I said, "Yes sir." I left to get everyone saddled up and ready as it was getting late in the day.

When we arrived I assigned a track to each corner of the bridge. The bridge was only about 45 meters across and the banks of the river were steep. In most places, it was about 20 feet straight down to the water. On each corner of the bridge, there was about a two-acre patch of pineapple plants. Out past the fields was all jungle. I positioned one mortar track on the southeast corner of the bridge and the other one on the northeast corner.

It was getting late quickly and I told every squad leader to hurry up and set up the RPG screen, set out two rows of claymore mines, dig an M60 machine position, and put out a row of trip flairs. I had told all of the squad leaders what the intelligence was about blowing up the bridge and everyone was pretty scared.

I assigned my squad members jobs to do and told them to hustle because it isn't long until dark. I knew that my men were scared, so I told them that I would go out and set the row of trip flairs because it was the most dangerous because you had to go out about 80 meters from the tracks. Since it was almost dark I told my squad, I'm going to be way out in front, so no matter what happens don't shoot until I get back in. I set out seven trip flares all across the front of our positions. When I was setting out the last one it was so dark that I couldn't see the little catch in the grove that set the pull trigger, so I let up on the handle of the catch slowly and I thought I felt it catch, when I let go the white phosphor flair went off in my hand. I jerked my hand away as fast as I could but it burned pretty badly. The skin on my hand was black and it was pretty painful. I yelled at my men, "DON'T SHOOT IT'S ME!" and I hustled back in. Our medic came to take care of my burn. He had some kind of red-colored anti-burn cream that was in his pack. He put a thick layer on my hand and bandaged my whole hand. The burn cream instantly made the pain go away.

I got the captain on the radio and told him that a trip flair had gone off in my hand and burned it pretty bad. He said, "Did the medic take care of your hand?" I told him yes he did a good job, it's not hurting. He asked me which hand was it, and I told him that it was my right hand. He said, "You are left-handed aren't you?" I said, yes sir. He asked me if I could shoot my M16 with my left hand and I told him that I had done it before. He said, "I need you to stay if you think that you can make it." I told him that I could make it.

Right at dark, we were all set up and I got all squad leaders on the radio and told them that we would be on 100% alert all night and no sleep and fire at any movement that you see or think you see. I told them that I would give them one-minute notice before every mad minute, and for the mortar tracks to put one 82MM round about 120 meters on each corner of the bridge every mad minute, and drop one round in the river at the bend above and below the bridge. It was about 200 meters to the sharp bends in the river both above and below the bridge.

One thing we didn't have to worry about with mechanized infantry was running out of ammo. We carried many cases of ammunition in our tracks. At random all night I called for mad minutes and I also told the mortar squad leaders that they could drop rounds at random all night. I think that I called for nineteen mad minutes that night. I didn't have to worry about anyone going to sleep, because all the soldiers understood the dangerous situation that we were in.

When daylight appeared and we were not attacked we thought that maybe intel about blowing up the bridge was wrong. But, when we went out to take up our claymores and trip flairs we found out that was wrong all of the trip flairs and trip wires were gone and all of our claymore mines were turned around towards us! If we had blown our claymores the 700 steel balls in each one would have come at us. I believe that the NVA was planning to attack us and blow up the bridge. When you saw that the claymores had been turned you kinda felt the hair on the back of your neck stand up. I believe that all of the mad minutes at random and the mortar fire changed the enemy's mind.

I got the captain on the radio and I asked him what our orders for the day were. He said, "Stay at the bridge until 1200 hundred hours and then I'll notify you what to do." One thing that we did while we were waiting for noon was to go fishing! A lot of soldiers liked to fish, including me and most of us hadn't been fishing in five or six months. They talked me into letting four of them throw hand grenades into the river to see if they could kill any fish. I finally agreed, but I said, "Be sure, and don't hit the bridge!" I told everyone to throw the grenades in the river on the count of three. Guess what? The soldier on the left by the bridge missed the water and his grenade landed on the bridge. Everyone hit the ground as fast as possible and we were lucky that no one was hit by shrapnel from the grenade. We retrieved three dead fish from the river and Ringo said that he would cook them for us.

We took an empty 50-cal ammo can and boiled the fish. All squad members and our Cho Hoi scout got to eat some boiled fish. That was the only fishing that we did while we were in Vietnam or Cambodia.

After the captain called about noon and told us to come back to the company's logger site. When we arrived at the company site the head medic told me to leave the bandage on my hand for three more days. I did and when he removed the bandages I could hardly believe it. The black skin came off with the bandage and new skin was already growing back.

While we were at the bridge all the guys in the platoon talked about the things that they didn't like about our new Company

Commander. They didn't like that he volunteered us for every dangerous mission that came up. They said all he cares about is body counts, and he doesn't care whose body it is!

They were mad about the man with the baby that was wounded by our bombs and he wouldn't let us get the baby any medical help. Also, all of us were very upset that on about the fourth day in Cambodia we were on a mounted search and destroy mission when the lead track spotted some bunkers in the edge of the wood line just ahead of them. They stopped and notified the captain of what they saw and he ordered the tracks squad to get off and go check the area out. Specialists Harper was walking point and all of a sudden the NVA set off a command detonated mine right by him and then they opened up with AK47 fire. Harper was killed instantly. The two tracks that were toward the front opened up with their 50-cal and M60 machine guns. The captain ordered us to pull back so that we could regroup and plan an attack on the wood line. We backed up and moved to the other side of the clearing opposite the bunker system. All of the squad members that were on the ground made it back to their track except Harper. We spaced out on line where all tracks were facing the wood line. Then the captain gave the order to commence fire and we all started firing at the wood line which was about 100 meters away.

I was listening on the radio and I heard the captain calling for air support with Cobra gunships. They answered that there were two gunships in the area and that they should be at the station in about ten minutes. When the Cobras arrived, we stopped firing and the Cobras made several passes on the wood line while firing their rockets and mini-guns. After their second pass, we stopped receiving fire.

When the helicopters left we assaulted the wood line again and stopped the tracks just before we got to the wood line. The captain had everyone except the track drivers dismount and search the area for dead or wounded NVA soldiers. We found nine dead NVA soldiers and we drug them out to the edge of the clearing. Some members of the Specialist Harpers squad put his body in a body bag. He was missing his left leg which was blown off and away from the rest of the body. The captain was counting the V. C. bodies that we had drug out of the jumbled woods and he found Harper's leg and he counted it as another dead NVA. Someone saw him and said, "You found Harper's leg!" He said, "That's another V. C. leg." Several troops told him that it was Harper's leg but he wouldn't let them put the leg in the body bag with the rest of the body. Everyone was very mad about that!

All of the soldiers in our company were still very upset because of what happened to Sergeant Campbell and Specialist Rasmussen while I was gone to the LCLC school. They said that they were going out on an eight-man ambush and as they were moving from their staging area to the ambush site, they got ambushed. The NVA blew the ambush with a round command detonated mine that was similar to our claymores. Sergeant Campbell and Specialist Rasmussen were both hit in the legs with pellets from the mine. The squad returned fire and after a while, they stopped receiving incoming fire. Both wounded soldiers were bleeding pretty badly, but they were able to put tourniquets on both of them and it helped stop the bleeding.

One of the troops on the ambush got the captain on the horn and told him that they were in a bad situation and that they needed a dust-off for both wounded men and that they all needed to be rescued. In a few minutes, the captain called back and said no dust-offs were available. Then he asked to talk to Campbell and Rasmussen. He asked them if they could make it until morning. Of course, both of them said yes. All of the platoon members back at the logger site kept requesting to go in and get them out but the captain repeatedly said "NO" we'll get them out in the morning!

The troops said that when they went in the next morning that Sergeant Campbell and Specialist Rasmussen were dead. They had bled to death sometime during the night. All of the soldiers said that if we would have gone in and got them last night they both probably would be alive now. This one had the whole company really "Tee'd Off"

CHAPTER 34
The Rice Cache
Cambodia

One afternoon when we were in Cambodia we had set up a logger site for the night. It was a battalion-size logger because we were still doing mainly battalion-size operations. A Cambodian man came up to the Battalion Commander's track and told him that he hated the NVA for what they had done to his family and that he knew where a small base camp of the NVA was and that they had several big bags of rice for their provisions. He told the Colonel that he would lead us to the camp. The Colonel told him thanks and to be back in the morning and that he would send a detail in with him to check out the camp and to destroy the rice. Of course, our gung-ho Company Commander, whom none of us liked, found out about the operation and he volunteered Bravo Company for the job as soon as he heard what the mission was.

The next morning the CO sent a runner to us. The runner said, "The CO wants Sergeant Whalen, Sergeant Dailey, and Sergeant Winborn to report to his track." When we got to his track he told us to get the 2nd and 3rd squads of the 3rd platoon ready to go on a search and destroy operation. He told us that after the tracks dropped us off we would have to walk about eight or nine hundred meters on foot to get to the NVA camp. He said that he would be joining us on the mission.

We traveled quite a way through the jungle trails on the tracks and finally, the Captain's track stopped and we arrived at the trailhead that the Cambodian man had said that the NVA camp was on. The Cambodian man pointed to the trail and told our Chu Hoi Scout, Ringo, that it was the way to the NVA camp. The captain told me to pick someone to walk point. I knew that this could be a bad situation that we were walking into. So I picked Sergeant Winborn to walk point and I told him that I would walk double point with him. We had walked double point several times in bad-looking areas and it had worked out pretty well.

We started down the trail with sixteen troops and the Cambodian man and the captain. We took our time walking down the trail because it was an area that looked like we could be ambushed at any time. We had to check the ground for trip wires and the trees for antipersonnel mines that we had sometimes found in the trees in Cambodia.

After we had gone about eight hundred meters we stopped and whispered, "Do you smell that?" I said it smells like something is burning. Winborn said, "yea, I smell it too, and I also smell V. C." We moved slowly forward with the safety of our M16s on Rock and Roll (fully automatic). As we approached a curve in the trail we eased up to look around the bend and there was the camp. We stood there for a while looking for any movement, but we didn't see anything except a hooch that had open sides and a thatch roof. A cooking fire was out in front of the hooch and it was still burning. We slowly eased out into the opening. The clearing was only about thirty-five meters long and about twenty meters wide. We were on high alert because there were enemy troops in the area somewhere close.

There were five big hundred-pound bags of rice stacked on a bamboo platform not far from the fire pit. All of our men eased into the clearing and I quickly had them set up a defensive circle around the base camp.

The hooch was a sleeping area for what looked like a platoon of men, as there were thirty bamboo beds lined up in two rows of fifteen under the canopy. The captain told us to pour all of the rice out on the ground and kick it into the dirt. When we were dumping the last bag the captain told Sergeant Winborn to save about fifty pounds of rice to give to the Cambodian man who took us to the food cache. Winborn looked at me and rolled his eyes. I knew that he didn't want to carry fifty pounds of rice for about a mile out. He knew that carrying that much weight out was not good because of the dangerous situation that we were in and because it was so hot that we couldn't keep the sweat out of our eyes.

When we got ready to go back up to the trail I told Sergeant Dailey to take point and that Winborn and I would bring up the rear and keep watch behind us. As Sergeant Winborn and I were backing out of the clearing he said, "Man I hate to carry all of this weight out of here." I told him just dump about one-half of it out here and they won't know the difference. He dumped more than one-half of the rice out and we started back up the trail while keeping a strong eye on our back trail.

We scattered out the usual ten meters apart as we left the clearing. When we got about one-half of the way back to the tracks, it was so hot that the CO had called a halt to rest and cool down, Winborn and I caught up with the rest of the troops and we picked a place to sit down in the defensive circle. The captain noticed that Sergeant Winborn didn't have very much rice in the sack. He said, "Winborn did you dump some of the rice out?" Sergeant Winborn answered, yes it was so heavy that I couldn't be ready to fight if we got hit. The captain told him to get his butt back to the NVA camp and get some more rice for the man.

Winborn looked at me and I told him that I would go with him. I felt like I was partly responsible for him dumping some of the rice out so I couldn't let him go alone. We walked side by side, back to back as we worked our way back to the NVA base camp. We both had our safety off and were ready for anything. When we approached the clearing we were very quiet and looked and listened for any sound or movement. We didn't see or hear anything so we moved up to the pile of rice that he had dumped out. I squatted down on one knee to watch for him while he raked rice into the bag as fast as he could. The trail on the opposite side of the clearing made a curve before it got to the clearing just like the curve on the side that we came in on.

Just as Winborn was tying the top of the bag of rice, I started hearing voices coming from the direction of the trail on the other side of the clearing. Winborn whispered, "Is it VC?" I answered, yea they're coming. Just as we stood up to get out of there I saw legs coming into view on the trail. Winborn dropped the bag of rice and we both dropped to one knee and flipped the safety off of our weapons. Three NVA came around the curve into full view about twenty-five meters from us. They had their AKs slung across their shoulders and when they saw us they started grabbing for their AKs. We both opened up with twenty-round bursts and got all three of them before they could get their weapons up. We both slapped in another magazine and Winborn grabbed the bag of rice and we hauled out of there as fast as we could. We were running because we didn't know how many more V. C. were coming. When we caught up with the rest of the mission troops that were still in the rest area we were soaking wet with sweat. We told them what had happened and that we didn't know if the NVA was following us or not. The captain gave the order to move out and believe me everyone was hot-footing it back to the tracks. We were glad to get out of that one alive.

CHAPTER 35

The Cloverleaf Cache
Cambodia

While we were in Cambodia nearly every day some kind of contact with the enemy occurred. We had penetrated about 20 miles of the country within about three weeks of the time that we invaded. We still had our company commander whom none of us liked.

We were checking out a new area trying to make contact with the enemy when a Cambodian man came up to the captain's track and said that he would show us a large cache where the NVA had stored many weapons and many boxes of ammunition. He got up on the captain's track and we moved out with him guiding us to the cache. You were always leery of someone telling you where to go and that they might be leading you into an ambush. So we were on high alert.

After about a two-mile trip through jungle trails and clearings, we arrived in the area where the man had said that the arms cache was located. We set all the tracks in a circle pointing out in a narrow clearing that joined two fairly large clearings together. From where my track was located I could look to the east and west and see most of both clearings. To our north and south was a thick jungle. A trail that came out of the jungle right next to my track was the one that the Cambodian man said led to the arms cache.

Then the captain sent out three 15-man patrols that were called Cloverleaf. They were to go out in three directions and make a big loop and then end up where they started and then do it again. The clover leaves went to our south, east, and west. The captain said for all platoon sergeants and track drivers to stay with the tracks and for one man to stay behind if there was not a platoon sergeant on the track. That way someone would be behind the 50-cal on all tracks. The rest of the company was to go with him to the cache.

Nick, my track driver, and I were trying to read some paper book westerns that someone had mailed to one of our guys. After about 15 minutes some of my squad started coming back to the track carrying new SKS rifles and P38 pistols that were still wrapped in wax paper. These were enemy guns that you could take home with you because they were not capable of fully auto and they were foreign-made. Throughout the year every man in my platoon got an SKS and a P38 pistol. I kept saying I'll take the next one, but the next one never happened. A couple of them brought back sealed cases of AK47 rounds. They were stored in sealed cans that looked like giant sardine cans. We put several cans in our track because we had several AKs stored in our track that we had taken from dead VC s. we kept the rounds because sometimes when we had a mad minute we would fire the AKs for the fun of it.

My men kept coming back with all kinds of weapons and ammo. They even found a case of potato masher grenades from the WWII era. They had German writing on them. Private Todd told me, you should see all of the stuff that's buried in a log-type cellar underground. I told him that I would like to see it and he said, "Go ahead, I'll set behind the 50-cal while you go look." I jumped down off the track and he climbed up. I asked him, "How do you get to the cache?" He said just follow the trail. I grabbed my M16 and a couple of bandoliers of ammo and started down the trail. He had told me that it was about 80 yards to the cache. I walked down the trail for quite a while and I saw about a 20-acre clearing ahead. I thought that must be it. I worked my way slowly up to the edge of the clearing and studied it. I saw no signs of anyone. The vegetation in the clearing had grown up to about waist high with a few banana trees scattered around the clearing that was about head high. I thought that I should have been at the cache before now, but I slowly started down the trail that ran down the middle of the clearing. By the time I was about 1/3 of the way across the clearing, I got a weird feeling that I was being watched. I felt the hair stand up on the back of my neck, and I knew that I had missed the cache and had gone too far. I hit the ground as fast as I could. I just knew that someone was watching me. I low crawled back to the wood line and then I worked my way back to the tracks. I told Private Todd what had happened and he said, "Oh yea, after about 50 meters you take a side trail to the west." I told him that I wasn't going to go again and that he could go back and help carry stuff. He started back down the trail and I got back behind the 50-cal. Nick was taking a little nap while he was setting in the driver's hatch.

I got in the 50-cal cupula and picked up the book that I had been reading and picked up where I left off. In all of the Louis Lamar westerns, there was always a big gunfight. I was just getting to the part about the gunfight. As I was turning the page I looked up and around me. In the clearing to the west of me, I could see the second platoon cloverleaf patrol moving through the middle of the clearing. The clearing was grown up like the one that I had low-crawled out of when I went looking for the cache. I started reading about the gunfight in the Riders of the Purple Sage when all of a sudden bullets started cracking all around me. I quickly looked to the east where the rounds were coming from and I saw the men in the cloverleaf hitting the ground and firing at the wood line to the east. I reached down and tapped Nick on the side of the head and Yelled, "Let's go, Nick!" The sound of the rounds cracking all around us had already woke him up and he was already starting the engine. All four tracks in the 3rd platoon fired up and hit the clearing at full speed. We spread out on line and drove up to where our guys were on the ground. Just as we were getting there the CO called and said 3rd platoon go help 2nd platoon they got hit. I already had my radio helmet on and I told him we are already there, sir. He said the rest of the company and I will be there shortly. I told the track commanders to open fire with the 50-cal machine guns. We pulverized the wood line with 50-cal rounds. In about 5 minutes the captain and the rest of the company arrived on their tracks. The Captain's track pulled up to my left and the track Lieutenant Smith was on, pulled up to the right. The captain ordered us to fire some more into the wood line. We opened up with everything that we had for a minute. We didn't receive any return fire. No one in the Cloverleaf patrol got hit. They all made it to the ground before anyone could be hit. In any firefight, if you made it to the ground without getting hit you had a good chance of not getting hit. All the guys on the cloverleaf patrol mounted on their tracks and the captain gave the order to move forward, so all tracks moved up to the edge of the wood line. The captain ordered everyone on his track to dismount and look for bodies.

They were just inside the wood line right in front of my track and they found two spider holes that the NVA had probably gone down into after firing a 30-round clip at the patrol. When they said, we found some spider holes, the captain pulled out his 45-cal pistol and trotted to them with a raised pistol. They were only about 20 yards in front of us and we could hear every word that was said. The captain picked out a small framed soldier from the second platoon and told him to get a 45 and a flashlight and go down and check out the tunnel. The private said, yes sir, but let me frag it first. The captain said, "I gave you an order, now get it done!" The private repeated, "Yes, Sir, but let me frag it first." We all knew that the V. C. were down in the spider holes and we nearly always dropped a cook-off grenade in one before we sent anyone down to check. The captain then cocked his 45 pistol and stuck it to the side of the soldier's head and said, "This is the last time that I'm giving you a direct order, get your butt down in that hole." When he said that every man in the company aimed at the captain with their M16s. there was a moment of silence, and then Lieutenant Smith came on the radio and said alright guys if you are not going to shoot put them down. The captain heard it on his radio and he turned to look. He saw that every M16 in the company was aimed at him. He slowly lowered his pistol and walked back and got on his track. The guys on the ground dropped a hand grenade down each spider hole and we left the area and headed to our new logger site.

If the captain would have shot that private we would have filled him full of M16 bullet holes, and Lieutenant Smith knew it. That evening Lieutenant Smith reported what had happened to the Battalion Commander. The next morning the Battalion Commander, who was a full bird Colonel, arrived in his helicopter. He removed the captain, whom none of us liked, from his command. The Colonel brought a temporary replacement CO with him until a permanent captain could be appointed. The Battalion Commander took the captain that he removed from command on the chopper with him and they lifted off and left. We were very glad to get rid of him. He had got some of our men needlessly killed.

CHAPTER 36

The "L" Shaped Clearing Bunker New Guy

We had been in Cambodia for thirty-one days and all of my platoon members were becoming combat-hardened soldiers. We were working in an area about twenty-five kilometers inside Cambodia and just on the east side of the huge Krek Rubber Plantation. We were told that the French owned the Rubber Plantation, but that they didn't live there anymore because of the war. They would pay the Cambodians to tap the rubber trees and collect the rubber sap and then they would come to get the product and ship it out.

That day we drove the tracks to an area that intelligence said had shown some enemy activity. The CO had us dismount except for the drivers and the 50-cal gunners. We were to go on a company strength straight leg patrol for three clicks through the jungle. The tracks were to back-track to an open area and then move into a large open area that went to our objective. They were to get there and then wait to pick us up when we got through the jungle area that we were supposed to check out.

The Company Commander told me to take my platoon and take point. My 3rd platoon seemed to be the one he picked to be point most of the time. I picked one of my squad leaders that I had walked point with many times. Sergeant Winborn was from Oklahoma like me and we trusted each other's instincts and decisions. When we walked point together one of us might see something that the other one missed, so double point worked out pretty well.

One of my guys got his 365 days in and went home. We all high-fived him and wished him well. The next day we got a replacement for him. He seemed like a good kid, really likable and ready to move out. The new guy asked if he could walk behind us. I told him yes, just be alert and be ready to hit the ground at the first sound of anything. Behind him were my RTO and the rest of the company were strung out ten meters apart. There were about sixty soldiers in the column and the length of the column reminded me of the eighty-man ambush that I took out at the end of the Lightening Combat Leaders Course. There was about a 600-meter column following us through the jungle.

We had walked through the jungle for about two hours when we came upon an "L" shaped clearing that was about 75 yards long on the short side of the "L" and about 120 yards long on the long side. The long side of the "L" was gradually uphill and the short side was down on level ground. The clearing had foliage that was knee-high to waist-high. Winborn and I had seen this kind of clearing before. It looked to both of us that the clearing had just been made for an ambush site. We were being very careful and stayed just inside the wood line and not out in the open as we crossed the short side and worked our way up the hill. We were almost to the top of the hill where the end of the clearing was and the jungle began again.

Winborn and I stopped to survey the surroundings before we moved out again I looked back down the hill at the short side and I could see that the troops had left the jungle and were walking along the wood line out in the open. They said later that they got out in the open because they were tired of fighting the jungle. That's what happens when you don't take every day like it's the only one that you have to live through. Winborn and I whispered to each other, "They should have stayed inside the wood line as we did." We moved up about 10 meters again and stopped. We were on the left edge of the clearing just barely inside the wood line. We were scanning the area for anything out of the ordinary. We saw something that didn't look right in the middle of the edge of the woods about 10 yards up the hill from us and 20 yards to our right. We were whispering to each other, it that a camouflaged bunker? If it is they have a full view of the short side of the "L" below. About that time some limbs and leaves were knocked out of the firing hole in the bunker and a machine gun opened up from what we thought was a hidden bunker.

We flattened out on the ground because we first thought that they were firing at us, but we soon realized that they were firing at the GIs down at the bottom of the hill that was out in the open. The new replacement private low crawled up to my right side while staying as low as he could, and Sergeant Winborn was on my left. We whispered to each other, "It's just a short matter of time until they see us and they will rip us to shreds." The private whispered that he thought he could get a frag in the firing hole of the bunker. We knew that we didn't have much time so I whispered, are you ready? He answered, "I have a grenade ready." I said, three Winborn and I opened up and the kid raised to throw his grenade. We were putting heavy fire into the hole, but the angle that we had was not good for the rounds to go everywhere inside the bunker. Just as the new guy's arm was coming forward they shifted the fire from the machine gun over to us. Just as he released the hand grenade he was hit three times, but like a miracle, the grenade bounced two times and went right into the firing hole of the bunker and blew up. Winborn and I rushed over to the bunker and we each emptied a magazine of ammo into the bunker to make sure that the threat was over. We immediately went back to the new guy and checked out his wounds. He took one round through a rib on his right side and one through his right forearm and one through the edge of his right shoulder muscle. While we were checking him out my radio operator crawled up and I got on the horn and told the Company Commander that I have a wounded man up at the point and that we needed a medic and dust off chopper. We all carried a couple of bandages with us, so Winborn and I put tight bandages on the arm wounds to help stop the bleeding. The CO called back and a medivac was on the way and the medic was coming up the hill. He told us as soon as the medic stabilized him for us to bring the wounded man to the bottom of the clearing where the ground is flat enough for the helicopter to land. He said that the rest of the company was setting up security around the landing area. Then he asked me if there were any enemy KIA's and I said, "Yes Sir, I counted three!"

The medic came up the hill as fast as he could and cleaned the wounds with antiseptic and put better bandages on all three of the private's wounds. Winborn and I walked him down to where the chopper could land and waited with him. He was in good spirits and we tried to reassure him that he would be alright. We talked about his hand grenade throw, and what a lifesaving miracle it was with him being hit just as he threw it, and for it to bounce right into the bunker hole anyway. We told him "You saved some lives today buddy." Only one trooper that was fired on first got hit, but it was a minor leg wound. Winborn and I both recommended him for a medal for valor. The dust off arrived and we loaded him on it and waved goodbye and good luck to him.

We still had several days to go in Cambodia and we had no way of checking on his condition. We never saw or heard of the new guy again. We hoped that he recovered from his wounds and that he would get to go home after that. He deserved it. We hoped that his three days in the field with us was all he would have to do.

CHAPTER 37

Lightning and Fate

S ome people say that fate is just good or bad luck, and some say that it is all in the plan and is divine intervention. I believe that it is the latter. I saw many bad things during my tour of duty and many incidents that you couldn't explain. If you used all of your talents and tried as hard as you could you probably had the best chance for you and your men to survive. But when a squad leader or platoon sergeant, that was very good at his job, got killed you wondered if it was meant to be regardless of how good he was. Was it fate or divine intervention or some of both? Even though you wondered, if you were a good leader and that the men respected you, you would still try your best to not get anyone and yourself killed or wounded regardless of fate or divine intervention.

In Cambodia, we worked our way as far as the huge Krek Rubber Plantation. There were miles and miles of rows of rubber trees. Someone told us that it was the largest rubber plantation in the world. The tops of the trees canopied over and there were straight roads in squares every square mile. Under the canopy it was like twilight when you were back in the trees and as the sun lit the roads they looked like streaks of spotlights with the sun shining through them. We went on many daytime ambushes the week that we were in the area. My ambushes never saw any enemy, but the first platoon had blown two ambushes during the week that we were in that area.

The rainy season was just beginning and it had stormed and rained for the last four evenings. The only action that we had was when I had an eight-man daytime ambush set up at one of the intersections of roads on the plantation. We had been set up for about an hour when we started hearing voices coming from up the trail from the south. We thought that it was enemy troops coming so we got ready. We had claymores set up on the edge of the road. Some were facing up the road, some down, and some pointing across the road. I whispered to everyone to be ready to blow their claymores when I blew mine. We were ready. The voices got louder and we knew that it wouldn't be very long before they came into view. When we saw them we looked at each other and we couldn't believe what we saw. It was two young Cambodian women that were carrying clay water jugs on their heads. They were pretty women and they didn't have anything covering their tops. We were silent and never moved a muscle and were hoping that they would pass on by without seeing us. We didn't know if they were associated with the enemy or not. When they were right in front of us one of them looked in our direction and made eye contact with us. She abruptly stopped and froze in her tracks. You could see the fear on her face. She quickly said something to the other one and they quickly turned around and walked back the way they came from as fast as they could.

After they were out of sight we had a quick discussion as to whether they might give our position away to the NVA. I told the men to go out one at a time and take up their claymores, and that we are going to move just in case. When everyone was ready we moved about one hundred meters back down the road in the direction that the women had come from. We quickly set out our claymores and got hidden as best we could and waited. After about three hours' no one came so we decided that they were just good Cambodian women going for water.

We were not supposed to stay for the night so we loaded up and started back to the battalion logger site. We were very cautious all the way back and we made it to the site without any trouble. The next day the whole battalion packed up and moved back towards the Vietnam border. We set up in one of our old logger sites which was only about three miles into Cambodia. There were about three inches of water on the ground after the monsoon rains hit that evening. The ground in that area was so flat that the water stayed on for quite a while. That was the reason that all of the Cambodian houses in the area were built on stilts.

After we set up in the logger site with Alpha and Charlie companies it started thundering and lightning again. Then the heavy rain hit again. A little after dark I was in the fifty caliber cupula on the track on guard duty. I had my radio helmet on and I was listening to the conversations. A tracked duster, which was a tracked assault vehicle with 40-cal Ack Ack guns instead of 50-cal machine guns, was lost from their unit and they asked if they could spend the night in our logger site. The Battalion Commander told them to come on in and find a spot on the perimeter and set up. About five minutes later they came in and passed by the back of my track and found a spot one track down from my left. It was still pouring down rain and lots of thunder and bad air-to-ground lightning when they stopped. I was looking at their track in the flashes of lightning and I saw three of the men climb out of the hatch and stand on top of their track, about that time a big bolt of lightning hit the radio antenna on top of the track. All three of them were killed by the lightning. The medics tried to revive them, but they were gone. We put them in body bags and loaded them back into their vehicle. The next morning a dust-off helicopter came and picked up the bodies.

After the heavy rain the night before the water level on most of the ground was three or four inches deep. We were supposed to go on a battalion-size search and destroy mission that day. When we were ready the Battalion Commander told Bravo Company to take the lead. We were loggered in a field that was next to a cart path that was as straight as an arrow and when you looked up or down you could see for about six hundred meters in both directions.

The Company Commander called me and said, "Sergeant Whalen, take the third platoon and take the point." My track would be the point track. Just as we started to make a sharp turn out of the field to get on the cart path our right track broke a link. I called the CO and told him that we had broken a track. He said, "Can you fix it?" I said, I think so, it was just one link that broke. He told me to get at it as soon as we could. As the squad members were trying to repair the track they ran into problems with one bolt. We were still working to fix it when the Battalion Commander came on the radio and told Charlie Company to go around Bravo Company and take the lead and for Bravo to catch up when the track was fixed. There was barely enough room for their tracks to get around mine in the small opening by the cart path, but they made it.

Just about the time we got the track repaired we heard a tremendous explosion down the cart path and lots of firing. There were several explosions and two really big ones. We ran out to the cart path and looked down the road and we could see that the lead two tracks had cooked off and exploded. They had been hit with numerous RPGs and the ammunition inside the tracks had cooked off and the tracks exploded. Two complete squads were instantly killed by the RPGs and exploding tracks. The rest of Charlie Company was firing everything that they had into the close wood line on both sides of the path.

The Battalion Commander called me and asked if we had the track repaired yet and I told him that we had just finished. He told me to take the point for Bravo Company and move down the path to help them. By then all of the firings had stopped. When we got to the exploded tracks he ordered us to dismount and do cloverleaf on both sides of the road. We found one dead NVA right in the ditch fairly close to the second track that had blown up. We looked at him and one half of his head was blown off. There was an RPG launcher beside him and we figured out that he had the launcher on the wrong side of him and that the gas escape hole was by his head and he had accidentally killed himself by making that mistake. He was the only dead NVA that we found.

After our cloverleaf didn't find any enemy the Battalion Commander told us to move down the trail past Charlie Company and set up security and for Alpha Company to stop before they got to Charlie Company and set up security. I had everyone in my platoon dismount and set up fighting positions on both sides of the trail and for the track driver and 50-cal man to stay on the tracks. After the dust-off helicopters arrived we could see them loading the body bags on to the helicopters from the dead on the two-point tracks that cooked off. None of the other Charlie Company men were hit.

After about an hour we were given the order to mount up and move out. We were to go to the next open area and spread out and wait for the rest of the battalion to get there. Thought-out the day we swept through several areas but we never made contact with any of the enemy. About the fourth big clearing that we come to we set up a new logger site for the night. The monsoons moved in again that evening and the next morning the whole ground looked like a lake.

We were ordered to move out back the way that we had come from with my track in the lead. We weren't given any instruction other than to go back. When we got back to our original logger site he told us to keep going and that we were pulling out of Cambodia because of the rainy season. On the way out I wondered why my vehicle had thrown a track the day before. Was it fate or divine intervention? Or was it just not our time to go?

Believe it or not, when we crossed the pontoon bridge back into Vietnam everybody cheered. We had been in Cambodia for forty-six days and had seen a lot of combat. My platoon of eighteen and nineteen-year-old soldiers came out of Cambodia as hardened combat soldiers.

We arrived at Tanyon instant airstrip at about 11:00 a.m. and were given the day off for some rest and to resupply everything that we needed. Our forty-six days of combat were over.

CHAPTER 38

The People of Cambodia

C rossing the bridge into Cambodia was like going into another world. There was a lot of different foliage, different terrain, and completely different people. The most notable thing was the people. The Cambodian people were good and likable. Once the Cambodians found out that we were not going to harm them, they worked with us every day because they didn't like the way the NVA soldiers treated them.

When we were driving our tracks across the country a lot of the Cambodian people would come out and wave hello to us. Many times they would toss pineapples up to us. The pineapples there were the best that I had ever tasted. Also, the ripe bananas picked from the stalk were the best I had ever tasted. I practically lived on them for the first few days that we were in Cambodia.

Sometimes when they would throw us pineapples we would throw them a can of C-rations, which was food new to them.

The houses in the area of Cambodia that we were in were all built on stilts because of the water that covered almost all of the ground during the rainy season. Everything in their houses was made from thatch and bamboo. They were self-sufficient. They grew their crops, hunted in the jungle, and picked fruit from the jungle. I never went into a Cambodian house that had any manufactured items. The only manufactured items that they had was their clothing. The clothing that they wore was all a type of gingham. All of the people in an area wore the same color and size of checks in the gingham. Three or four miles away the people would all have a different color of gingham. We figured that the different colors designated different family units.

I remember thinking that these people don't need much of a government because of the self-sufficient lifestyle that they lived. I figured that these people had lived this way for centuries. They just wanted to be left alone.

★　　★　　★

CHAPTER 39

R & R in Cu Chi
at Waikiki East

After we returned from forty-six days in Cambodia we were ordered to go to Cu Chi for a two-day rest time. An in-country R & R center was established for troops who had been in extended combat operations. The name of it was Waikiki East. It consisted of barracks with bunks, a small black and white TV, a basketball court, and a small stage for floor shows.

The officers brought in a pickup bed trailer full of iced-down beer and several cases of all kinds of liquor. It was the first iced beer that we had seen in months. Once a week we would get one case of hot beer for each squad in the company. Hot beer didn't go over very well with the boys that drank it.

There were showers in a small hooch, and the first thing that most of us did was take a shower. We sometimes would go two or three weeks without any kind of washing up while out in the field, because when you are in a combat situation being dirty, "doesn't mean nothing!" Just living. We did occasionally take showers by putting a water can on top of the track then stripping off Jaybird naked and soap up while another soldier controlled the flow of the water. We didn't wear any underwear or socks because every day we would get our clothes soaking wet either by sweat or monsoon rain, and our clothes would dry out faster without getting galled and or blisters. Sometimes we could take fatigues off and they would almost stand up by themselves. So we were really glad to get to take an actual shower.

After we had settled in most of the troops got loop-legged drunk. Sergeant Calhoun and I picked out two side-by-side bunks to lay back on and watch TV. We were just happy to be alive. We had been watching TV and talking for about an hour when one of our guys in our platoon came stumbling by. He had a full bottle of Seagram's 7 and a bottle of Crown Royal. He was a happy drunk. He stopped at the end of our bunks and said, "You all sergeants want a bottle?" We both said, no we're alright, but he staggered up to the little table that was between our bunks and set down the bottle of Crown Royal, and he staggered away. He said, "You sergeants drink up now, that's an order." We laughed about him giving us an order.

We continued to watch TV and talk for a while and Sergeant Calhoun picked up the bottle of whiskey and looked it over. Then he said you want a shot of this. I said to him, maybe one shot, how about you? As Sergeant Calhoun opened the bottle he said, "Yea, just one shot." After a while, we were passing the bottle back and forth. We realized that we had emptied the bottle and were very drunk.

We could hear guys playing basketball on the outside court. Calhoun asked me if I played basketball. I told him basketball was my favorite sport to play and that I had played basketball from 5th grade through Junior College. He said let's go out there and beat those guys. Six black brothers were playing and we asked them if we could play and they said, yea – come on. They were about as drunk as us. The dirt court was muddy from recent rain, as the monsoon season was starting to move in. We played for about an hour and it was fun. You would go in for a layup and fall flat on your face in the mud. By the time we all decided that we had had enough of the mud bowl. We were all covered with mud. We went to the showers and show-ered with our fatigues on to get the mud off of us and our clothes. I still remember the fun we had that night in "the mud bowl."

The next morning at Waikiki East R & R center we were assembled by our captain and told that there would be a floor show on stage at 17:00 hours and that we could go to the PX, shopping, post office, barber shop, and try to call home if we wanted to. He instructed us which building to go to if we wanted to try to call home. The only way you could call was by radio. Every time you said something to the person that you called you had to say over so that the radio operator that was listening to your conversation could switch to the other person. I waited in line for about an hour to get a chance to call my wife, and I finally got to call her. Before they let her talk to me they had instructed her on how to talk on the radio. I was only allowed 5 minutes to talk because there were so many more waiting to call home. They instructed us at the assembly that morning that if we did call home and got through. We were not to say our rank, where we were, or where we thought we were going to be. Five minutes didn't last very long because of the time consumed by the radio operator to change us back and forth. But, I was very happy to hear my wife's voice and ask how she and our baby girl was doing, and to tell her that I was okay and to find out that they were okay.

At about 4:30 p.m., we started filling the chairs in front of the stage to get ready to see the floor show. It would be the first and probably only show that we would see in Vietnam. Bob Hope had been there about a month ago, and the only troops that got to see the big shows were people assigned to the rear areas, not combat troops. The night Bob Hope was there, we were out in the Iron Triangle on nighttime ambush.

The floor show that we saw was an all-girls South Korean band. They put on a pretty good show. The songs they sang were all American songs that we all knew. The main two songs that they sang were: Rolling on the River, and Like a Bridge over Trouble Water.

All the songs were sung with a strong Asian accent. All in all, it was a good short rest.

The next morning, we resupplied the tracks with cans of diesel, ammunition, water, and cases of C-rations. We then returned to our area of operations in the Iron Triangle. Back to the grind.

★ ★ ★

CHAPTER 40
The Skull

We were sent back into an area where we had worked about three months ago. It was in the Northwest part of what was known as The Iron Triangle. Our mission was to do search and destroy missions in the daytime and then to pull security for a small fire base at night. We would do the usual and send out three eight-man ambushes at night. The tracks and the rest of the troops in the company would stay in the firebase to help secure it.

On the day that we arrived, we checked in at the firebase and then went on a mounted search and destroy mission. While on the mission we came upon an area that had several V. C. skeletons that were completely clean of flesh and were bleached white by the sun. the Viet Cong hardly ever buried any of their dead comrades. After about four or five days in the hot sun and the maggots, the skeletons would be bleached clean.

One of the second platoon tracks was in front of mine. They stopped and a soldier jumped off of their track and walked over to a skeleton and picked up a skull. Then he climbed back upon the track with the skull. Our Chu Hoi scout, Ringo, was on my track and when he saw the kid take the skull from the rest of the body, he said, "Boo-Cu Bad, Boo-Cu Bad." I asked Ringo why it was bad. He said, "It's religion, if the head is removed from the body upon death, his soul wonders forever, he can never be reborn." A major religion in Vietnam believed in reincarnation. One of my squad leaders and I talked about how scared Ringo was when he saw the skull removed from the body of a dead Viet Cong. We decided to start doing whatever it took to try to stay alive and to do something that may help keep us and our men alive. We both wrote to our wives and told them to find the biggest bowie knife that they could find and to mail them to us as soon as possible.

We didn't make any contact with the enemy on our patrol so we returned to the firebase. The firebase was not a new one. It had been there for some time. It had a berm around it and evenly spaced sandbagged bunker fighting positions, also around the berm. Because of the sand-bagged bunkers, we didn't have to dig any fighting positions that evening. The bunkers also had three layers of sandbags on top to guard against mortar rounds.

When we got our tracks in the position we set out rows of trip flairs, and claymore mines, and set up the rocket screen in front of all of the tracks. The rocket screen was chain link fencing and two metal poles to hold it. If an RPG was shot at the track it would hit the fence and blow up and not do as much damage to the men or the track as a direct hit would.

The three ambushes got saddled up and left on foot to get to their ambush coordinates about thirty minutes before dark. It was not my turn to take an ambush out so I stayed with the track for security. We set up our M60 machine guns in the bunkers on both sides of my track. We ate a box of C-rations and then assumed our fighting positions for the night. We would all take turns rotating behind the 50-cal on the track throughout the night.

The second platoon's positions were to the left of my track. One of the bunkers on the second platoon track that was immediately to the left of mine was occupied by the soldier that picked up the skull and by one of his squad members. He placed the snow-white skull on top of the berm directly in front of their position. It shined like a light. I didn't think that it was a good idea to do that. It would turn out to be a very deadly idea.

About thirty minutes after dark all three ambushes had just called in negative sit-reps when a trip flair went off out in front of the second platoon squads position. Then immediately an RPG flashed through the air and made a direct hit on the bunker with the skull. Both guys in the bunker were instantly killed by the explosion. Then the whole base was hit on two sides with RPGs and automatic weapons fire. Then they started dropping some 81-millimeter mortar rounds inside the firebase. We opened up with everything that we had on the wood line in front of us. You could see our 50-cal machine gun tracer bullets popping in one side of trees and out the other. Our mortar tracks started dropping 82-millimeter mortar rounds all around the outside of the berm. The 155-millimeter tracked artillery dropped their barrels as low as they could and started firing flechette rounds into the wood line. The flechette rounds were like a giant shotgun firing many projectiles.

We believed that we were being hit by a fairly large force of the North Vietnamese Army. The Commanding Officer got on the horn and called for helicopter gunship support and Phantom Jets with napalm. There were two of us in each bunker, one with an M16 rifle and the other with an M60 machine gun. I was in the fighting position on the left side of my track. I was slapping a new magazine into my M16 and I saw an RPG streaking out of the wood line it hit the rocket screen in front of my track and exploded. The shrapnel went through the wire and hit the front of my track and went all the way through the front of my track and out the back. Private Andretti was on the track firing the 50-cal and his ears were ringing, but he never got hit by any of the shrapnel. We were lucky that the shrapnel that hit the track didn't hit any of the ammunition that was stacked inside the track. If they had been hit it could have resulted in a cook-off and would probably have killed all of us in the area.

Two Cobra gunships were the first air power to arrive on the scene. They made firing runs on both of the sides that we were receiving fire from. They came in with mini-guns blazing and rained rockets down on the wood line in front of us. We stopped receiving any fire after they had made their second pass. About that time the Phantoms arrived on the scene with their napalm canisters. The helicopters left and the jet pilots dropped napalm on all four sides of the firebase. They were so close that when they exploded the wind sucking to the napalm would almost pull you down.

After the jets left the fight was over. The firefight lasted about twenty-two minutes. The only casualties that we had were the two GIs in the bunker with the skull. They were both killed with the first RPG that hit right inside their bunker. We were on full alert for the rest of the night, but no attacks occurred. The choppers and jets with napalm did their job.

When it got light all three ambushes came in and said that they didn't see any movement all that night. They said that the V. C. must have taken a different trail than the ones that their ambushes were set up on. We went out to count V. C. bodies the next morning and there were many. Most of the dead were burned black by the napalm. A dust-off chopper came to pick up the bodies of the two GIs that were killed. Andretti and I helped load the body bags on the chopper.

At about 10:00 a.m. we mounted up and moved out for a daytime search and destroy mission. During the day we checked out many areas. There was a fresh sign of enemy troops, but we didn't find any. Later in the afternoon, we set up a logger site about two miles from the firebase. I took out one of the three ambushes that night. We were almost certain that we would make contact with the enemy because of the large number of enemy troops in the area that had attacked the fire base the night before. We were on full alert the whole night, but nothing ever showed up. The other two ambushes had the same story. So, what was left of the enemy force must have withdrawn to a completely different area.

When we received our big bowie knives in the mail we decided how to use them for the best effect. We used them as machetes to chop a way through thick jungle and to remove some heads from dead VC.

We had unit crest pins with our company insignia that had two sharp pins that were supposed to go through your uniform and a keeper would go on the back of the crest to hold it on. The insignia on our tracks was a white diamond with a "2" in each corner. We would put one of the pins on the forehead of a dead V. C. and tap it hard with the butt of our hand. When the body melted away in the heat, the skull would be away from the body with our unit crest stuck in the forehead. The Viet Cong and the North Vietnamese Army would know who killed them.

After about a month of doing the unit crest thing our first platoon got a new Chu Hoi scout. He had read one of our Chu Hoi leaflets that our planes dropped all over the country to try to get some enemy troops to come over to our side. The leaflets said surrender, and come over to our side. You will be treated well with plenty to eat and drink. Ringo, my Chu Hoi scout was talking to the new scout. He told Ringo that the VC and the NVA were very afraid of the white diamond because they would take the head. When he told Ringo that he made a motion with his finger from one ear to the other. He said, "Boo Cu Bad, Boo Cu Bad."

We didn't know for sure but we believed that our bowie knives and crests probably saved several GI's lives.

CHAPTER 41
R & R in Hawaii

After you had been in Viet Nam for six months or more you qualified for a seven-day leave. The purpose of the rest and relaxation was to let you unwind some from the stress of combat. Although even the support staff that never saw any combat got to go on R & R also.

Specialist John Brown and I put in for R & R at the same time and both of us were going to meet our wives in Hawaii. On the evening of the day before we were going to leave for R & R, we caught the resupply chopper back to Cu Chi. We caught another chopper to the Tay Ninh base just outside of Saigon our plane was to leave for Hawaii from there. We had four choices to pick from to where we were allowed to go on R & R. We could go to Germany, Australia, Hawaii, or Ban Cock, Thailand. We both chose Hawaii because it was a state and was the closest place for our wives to come to. When we arrived at Tay Ninh airstrip we were kinda apprehensive, because Tay Ninh was known as rocket city. It was called that because the V. C. would shoot V22 indirect rockets quite often at the airstrip and base there.

As John and I were walking from where we got off of the chopper to the R & R center people were walking all around. We saw two guys come out of a building dressed in white shorts and white t-shirts that were pulling golf club bags with rollers and were headed for the golf course to play golf. We froze in our tracks and just watched them go by. There we stood in our dirty combat fatigues that would almost stand up by themselves when you took them off and they were dressed like that and playing golf. John looked at me and said, "Do you believe that they are drawing combat pay." I answered, "We were out there killing V. C. and living in the dirt and they get to do this and draw combat pay!" When we got to the R & R center and started processing through they gave us a new dress uniform and medals to put on them. We were able to shower and shave and get ready for the trip.

The next morning a bus picked up all the troops that were going to Hawaii for R & R and some that were going home. The bus took us to the Bien Hoa airbase to board the jet to Hawaii. John and I had both written letters to our wives and gave them the date and the time that we would arrive in Hawaii. They had got plane tickets that would get them there at approximately the same time that we were to arrive there. My wife was bringing our daughter, Kim, with her to see me. It had been about seven months since I had seen them, and it seemed like it had been seven years to me.

The flight to Hawaii was uneventful and after several hours the pilot came on the intercom and told us to look out the windows to the right side of the plane to see the view of the Hawaiian Islands. We landed at the military airport and buses were lined up to take us to the reception center. John and I got on the front seat of the first bus in line and when the bus was loaded the driver pulled out for the reception area.

It was several miles to the reception center from the airport where we had landed and the driver drove in heavy traffic at about 65 miles an hour. We were holding on to the handrail with white knuckles because we hadn't been over thirty-five miles an hour on the ground for seven months. It looked to us like we were going ninety miles an hour. We didn't know what to expect at the reception center, but we were told that our loved ones would be there waiting for our arrival.

When the bus pulled up in a large parking lot at the reception center we saw two lines of women that were in a long line about five feet apart and about forty yards long. You could see them all waving, screaming, and yelling. It looked like they were in a frenzy. The driver popped the bus door open and said, "There they are. Go get 'em, boys!"

As we went down the line the girls were so frantic that some would grab you and kiss you, and then say oh I'm sorry, I thought you were him. John was ahead of me and we were about one-half of the way to the end of the line when his wife jumped out of the line and grabbed him. After I was grabbed about a dozen times by the time that I got to the end of the lines I was shaking like a leaf in a windstorm. When I got to the end of the line I looked around and my wife and daughter were not there. I didn't know what to do. Everyone who found their husband or boyfriend immediately left the area and all that was left in the area was four GIs and three girls. All of the girls started crying because they thought that their husbands or boyfriends had probably been wounded or killed in action. We tried to console them by telling them that their guys were probably on a later flight. About that time a man came out of the reception center and announced that one flight out of California had a thirty-minute delay and that it would be landing shortly. He said that if any of our people were on that flight that the buses would bring them to the reception center as soon as they disembarked the plane and got their luggage.

While I was waiting on my wife and daughter the three girls and the other three GIs whose loved ones didn't show up kinda paired up and gradually walked away together. About that time, I heard a bus pull up behind me and I turned to look. The door swings open and my wife stepped off and when we saw each other we ran to each other. At first, I didn't recognize my wife because when I left for Vietnam she had brown hair, now it was blonde. After hugging and kissing, I asked her, where is the baby? She said, she had a light fever and wasn't feeling good and I didn't want her to have a miserable trip, so I left her with your mother.

It was a wonderful feeling to see and be with my wife again. Many times I thought that I would never see her or my daughter again. We had a wonderful five days. We went to the beach several times and swam in the ocean. One day John Brown and his wife joined us on Waikiki Beach. We stayed for several hours out in the sun. John and I both had deep Vietnam sun tans, but our wives didn't. John's wife got a sunburn, but my wife got a severe sunburn that day and even got sick from it.

We walked around every night, and we heard Don Ho, the famous Hawaiian singer, sing and saw several luaus. Every day we ate different food at different restaurants. It was a wonderful time. I liked the fact that Hawaii didn't have mosquitoes and snakes. One of our days we took a bus tour of part of the island and saw the magnificent scenery. Another day we went to a sea life park and saw the show. We enjoyed watching the tricks that the porpoises and orcas did. On our last day, we went to the zoo. It was a very good zoo and we were enjoying watching all of the different animals. We had taken almost a whole roll of film up in my 35mm camera, and a few pictures on a smaller camera. While we were at the grizzly bear exhibit there were people everywhere around watching the bears.

There was a bench about two steps back from the bear fence and I set down to rest for a minute. My wife was still at the fence watching the bear. I set my camera down on the bench beside me. My wife turned to me and said, "Come and look what the big bear is doing now." So I stepped up to the fence to look at the funny moves that the bear was making and left my camera on the bench right behind me. I was probably up on the fence for about twenty seconds and I remembered my camera, so I turned around to get it. It was gone! I looked around with a quick look and I saw a young boy running through all of the people with my camera just as he went out of sight around the corner of a building I took off running after him. When I rounded the corner of the building there were people everywhere and I didn't see the boy anywhere. I didn't mind losing my camera as much as I did losing all of the pictures that we had taken on our first four days in Hawaii.

Our five days flew by, but they were magical times. It was time for me to leave and head back to Vietnam. I had to be at the bus pickup at 9:00 a.m. and my wife's flight home left a little later that day. One of the hardest things to do is to leave someone that you don't want to leave, especially knowing that it could be your last time to see them. We hugged and kissed goodbye and I got on the bus bound for the military airport. Shortly after our bus arrived at the airport we boarded a plane that was bound for Vietnam and John and I were on our way back to war.

CHAPTER 42
Back from R & R

It was very hard to leave my wife in Hawaii, but the days flew by and I had to go back. I was dreading it. I knew that I had five more months of trying to survive before I would have the chance to go home and see her and my daughter again. It was always in the back of your mind that no matter how hard you tried, you might not make it.

I arrived back at the company area in Cu Chi at about noon. First Sergeant Tinga told me that I could go back out on the resupply chopper that afternoon or if I wanted to I could catch a ride out on the mechanic track as it was leaving to go repair a track in about twenty minutes. I told him that I would ride out to the logger site with the mechanics. He told me that they were not a logger site, but that they were attached to an engineering company that was reconstructing the bridge that had been blown up by the VC and that they were staying in a firebase with the engineers.

I grabbed my M16 and three bandoleers of ammo, my little travel bag, and then I walked out to the motor pool where the mechanic tracks were kept. The mechanic squad was about ready to leave when I got there. I told them that I wanted to hitch a ride with them. The lead man said, "Glad to have you, jump on." I could smell strong marijuana smoke and I could tell that they were all high. We in the fighting platoons didn't stand for anyone in them to take or smoke any kind of drugs. The only ones that we saw that did, were the ones that were stationed in the rear areas and we didn't have any say over them.

I jumped on the right front side of the mechanic track and settled in, and all the mechanics sat all over the top of the big track, and we took off. They were a happy, carefree bunch, and I didn't feel very safe with them. I didn't see any weapons and I asked them if they had any. One of the guys said, "I think there is some inside the track man." I remember thinking, oh boy, I should have waited to come out on the chopper. It took us about three hours to get to the base camp, but about two miles before we got to the fire base we passed through a small town. The people would come out of their houses and look at us as we drove by. I didn't like the look on their faces. They didn't look that friendly to me! As we were passing through the town I looked at some hooches behind the first row of houses and I saw five men dressed in black pajamas with AK47s and they just looked at us as we passed by.

I said to the guy beside me, did you see those guys with the AKs back there? He said, "Yeah, man, that's a VC town, they are VC, but they usually don't bother you in the daytime." I thought to myself they probably don't bother these guys because they act so crazy yelling and hollering and revving up the diesel engines as they blew through the town.

When we arrived at the base I found my company area and reported to the Company Commander. He told me to settle in for the afternoon and that I would be taking out an ambush that night. I thought, "Back to the grind." No one had informed me that we were only a few miles from the Cambodian border and that we were working in an area of Nui Ba Den. I asked my scout, Ringo, what that meant in English and he said, "Black Virgin Mountain." It was a huge mountain in the middle of very flat land. The Black Virgin

Mountain was something to see. It just didn't look real, that a mountain that big would be just all by its lonely self but it was.

During the daytime, while we were pulling security for the engineers we went on patrols on all four sides of the construction site. At night we sent out four ambushes. One for each side of the bridge. If you didn't go on a nighttime ambush you got to stay with the company stationed in a nearby fire base with the engineer unit that was there.

We got to eat with them when we were not out on patrol or an ambush. We couldn't believe the quality of the meals that they had. They had everything for breakfast that you could think of and for the other meals, food such as steaks, seafood, pork chops, and many other good choices. We were used to living on canned C-rations and an occasional hot breakfast of powdered scrambled eggs, turkey bacon, and tang. We couldn't believe all of the good hot meals that they had, and every time that we had a chance to eat in their Chow Hall we took advantage of it. It was by far the best food that we had in Vietnam.

We pulled security for the engineers for three days and three nights before being relieved by our Charlie Company. During one ambush that I took out, the Viet Cong gave us a little probe by sneaking in and firing one burst of fire from an AK in our direction. We immediately returned fire and after a few magazines were fired by us there was no return fire. No one got hit by the fire because we were on the ground and the AK fire went over our heads. I think that they were just trying to see if we were alert.

When we left the area of the mountain we were sent back into the central part of our old operations area that was known as the Iron Triangle, we would kill or drive all of the enemies out of the area and then leave. A month or so later they would send us back to that area and it would be crawling with the enemy again. There was no strategy to take and keep areas that we had captured. It seemed like it was a never-ending cycle.

★　★　★

CHAPTER 43
The Death of Jim Johnson

Jim Johnson was a nineteen-year-old draftee just out of high school. He was a very likable guy and everyone got along with him very well. He looked and talked just like the movie star of the past era Robert Mitchum.

I was platoon sergeant when he was assigned to my platoon. I assigned him to the first squad of the third platoon. He had been there about three weeks and had been in a couple of firefights and had done his job well. Lieutenant Smith, our third platoon leader got his six months in the field in and he was assigned to a rear area job. Officers only had to serve six months in the field, and then the rest of their year tour of duty would be a rear area job.

The next day we got a new Lieutenant to be our platoon leader. He picked Johnson to be his radio man. The Lieutenant had been there about three or four days and we had seen enough out of him to see that he was dangerous, and too "Gung Ho." He didn't seem to sense or see danger as those of us that had been in combat many times did.

On the fatal day, my platoon was on a roving patrol search and destroy mission, when this Vietnamese kid stopped one of our tracks and told our Chu Hoi scout that he had found a mine in a small cart path road and that he would show us where it was at. The Lieutenant jumped right on it and he had us follow the kid with our tracks.

When the kid stopped we flicked the safety off our weapons because we had seen this before. Once a kid led us to what he said was an arms cache and pointed at the ground. When two soldiers squatted down to look he took off running and stopped and pulled a trip wire and the booby trap exploded and killed both of the men. We ripped him apart with our M16s and M60 machine guns. We thought that this situation looked very similar. The new Lieutenant jumped off of the track and looked back and said, "Johnson, come on." Then he turned to go to the kid who was about forty meters out front of us pointing at the ground. As Johnson was getting off of his track, several of us whispered to him, "Johnson don't go, stay here, that guy is going to get somebody killed." Johnson stopped. The lieutenant was about halfway to the Vietnamese kid when he looked back and saw that Johnson wasn't coming and he yelled, "Johnson, get your ass up here now!" Johnson looked at us and rolled his eyes and went to him. As the lieutenant knelt on the spot, I saw him pull a bowie knife out of a sheath on his belt to probe with. I knew that it was a mistake, we were trained to never probe in the ground with anything metal. We had whittled wooden knives out to probe with. The Lieutenant knelt and Johnson was standing directly behind him and the kid was in front of him. When he stuck the knife into the ground he must have touched both prongs of a battery with the blade because the mine exploded. It killed all three of them. The Vietnamese kid and the Lieutenant were severely torn apart, but Johnson only caught one piece of shrapnel that came through the lieutenant and hit him, but the projectile hit him directly in the chest and went right through his heart, and killed him instantly.

We had to put them in body bags as best as we could. I was in charge since the Lieutenant was killed so I had called a chopper to come and pick up the bodies or what was left of them. After we had loaded them on the chopper it went through my mind. He was a good man and a good soldier. What a waste to lose him, especially because of someone else's mistake!

CHAPTER 44

Direct Field Commission

A fter the death of our new Lieutenant and Private Johnson, there were no lieutenant officers available as replacements at the time. The second platoon, platoon leader got his six months in the field at about the same time as ours was killed, so we had two platoon leader jobs that were open. The captain picked me to be the acting platoon leader for the third platoon, and another sergeant from the second platoon to be acting platoon leader for them.

About three weeks had gone by and we hadn't received any replacement lieutenant. We had gone on several operations in that time frame and had some short firefights and booby trap experiences. One afternoon when we had set up our logger site for the night the captain called me and the other sergeant that was acting platoon lender to his track. It was usually an intelligence briefing that gave us the intel on enemy movement in the area and the coordinates of the night's ambush sites. But he told us that the Battalion Commander was on his way to meet with us.

When the Battalion Commander arrived we went to greet him by his chopper. We saluted him because it was a fairly safe area. Usually, you don't salute officers in the field because the enemy could be watching and then targeting them. He told us to stand at ease and that he had a proposition for us. He said both of you are being offered a direct field commission as a first lieutenant in the United

States Army. If you accept the commission the only person that can remove you from that rank is the President of the United States. Do you want to accept this appointment? I asked him, "Sir, what is the catch?" He said, "You will be expected to sign up for two more years in the Army." I told him that I had a wife and a child and if I get out of there alive I don't want to have to leave them again. I told him that I was honored to be recommended for a direct field commission as an officer, but that I respectively decline the offer. He tried to change my mind, but I told him that was my final decision.

The other sergeant from the second platoon was a single guy and he said, "I don't have a family of my own to worry about, so I will accept the appointment." I stayed as acting platoon leader for two more weeks and then we received a replacement Lieutenant for my job and I returned to my old job as platoon sergeant of the 3rd platoon of Bravo Company.

CHAPTER 45
Small Things

Rainy Season When the rainy season was on in Vietnam it would rain almost every evening. About 3:00 or 4:00 p.m. the clouds would start rolling in. The daytime temperatures would reach anywhere from 95-105 degrees every day. The humidity was terrible, and we had to wear Army towels around our necks to wipe the sweat out of our eyes. When the rain moved in some days there would be lots of thunder and lightning and others not so much. The rain usually lasted two to three hours, and then it would clear off and a strong wind would pick up. The temperature would drop from around 100 to about 65 degrees. If you were wet, you would get so cold from the wind and the drastic temperature change that your teeth would chatter. If it wasn't for the wool Army blankets, I think we would have got hypothermia.

When we went on nighttime ambushes during the rainy season if there was a cemetery close we would always set up in it. The reason was because the graves were elevated because of the water level during the rainy part of the year and we could sleep on them up out of the water. For some ambushes during the rainy season, we would have to set up in a rice patty. We would have to lay in the water for the whole night, and when it was your turn to sleep you had to put your M16 on your chest to keep it out of the water. We didn't wear any shorts or socks, especially during the rainy season because you would get galled because of the heat and moisture.

Showers, we never got to take showers very often. Sometimes during the rainy season in our logger site, we would strip off jay bird naked and soap up, and let the rain be our shower. During the dry season, we would use the six-gallon flat-sided water cans for a shower, but not very often. We figured out that dirt won't kill you, when we took our pants off they would almost stand up by themselves from the sweat, mud, and blood. One of the guys in our squad took a hammer and punch and put several holes in one of the flat-sided water cans and we would put water in it and lay it on top of the track to be our shower. It worked pretty well. One guy would be on top of the track to lay the can down when you needed water and set it up when you didn't so that we could save water.

Haircuts, when we got our third Company Commander his first order was for all of us to get a haircut. Most of us had quite a bit of hair because we hadn't been in any rear area for quite a while and had no opportunity to see a barber. All the soldiers in my platoon were griping about having to get a haircut while out in the field. One trooper had a pair of hair-cutting scissors and a big comb. He said, "Can anybody cut hair?" No one said anything, so I said, "Yeah, I can cut hair." So he handed me the scissors and comb and I asked who wants to be first. My wife was a beautician and I had watched her cut some people's hair with scissors so I thought that I could fake it and act like I knew what I was doing and cut their hair for them. While I was cutting I would make the scissors snap a lot so that it sounded like I knew what I was doing. Believe it or not, the haircuts turned out not so bad.

Steel Pot, the steel pot was issued to all infantry troops along with a jungle hat. Most troops chose to wear the jungle hat instead of the steel pot because they were cooler. I chose to wear the steel pot because I thought that there was a chance that it might save me from some shrapnel wound to the head. Also, I needed it after I became squad leader and platoon sergeant because at night when I called in helicopter gunships I would take the steel pot off and put my strobe light in it. The pilots could see it and know where my position was and the enemy couldn't see it. I could tell the pilot on the PRICK25 radio the direction that the VC or NVA was from my position, and they would know where to put their ordinance out without hitting friendlies. Steel pots were heavy to wear, but after a few days, you got used to it and didn't notice the weight.

Smoke Flairs, as a squad leader or platoon sergeant I always carried three colored smoke grenades. They were used to mark your position for aircraft in the daytime. The pilot of the jet or the helicopter would tell me to pop a smoke to mark my position. As soon as the smoke popped he would identify the color or colors that he saw. Many times the V. C. were listening on the radio and they would pop smoke when I did. Sometimes I had to pop another color of smoke and not tell the pilot that I was popping another smoke and then as soon as he saw the new smoke he would identify the color of the new smoke and then I affirmed that the color was me. Sometimes we had to do it this way to beat the enemy.

Suicide Mission, two days after the ambush that I was a part of that blew it on an 800-man NVA Battalion I was going on an ambush in the same general area. All eight of us were scared we knew that it could be a very dangerous area to be back into. Everyone was pretty solemn as we were saddling up getting ready to leave. Everyone was almost doubling the amount of grenades, claymores, and ammo that we usually carried on an ambush. We always carried more ammo than straight-leg infantry because we didn't have to carry it all the time.

The 3rd platoon tracks took us out to drop us off. We drove right by the area where we had blown the big ambush. About 300 meters away the platoon sergeant had the track stop for us to jump off. Seven of us jumped off track but one didn't. this guy was from Chicago and he refused to get off of the track. We were all whispering for him to get off the track. He started talking loud and yelling that it was a suicide mission and that he refused to go. We all told him to be quiet or he was going to get us all killed. He just got louder screaming the same thing over and over. As loud as he could yell he screamed, it's a suicide mission, I refuse to go. Send me to Long Binh Jail. I don't care! In unison, we all pointed our M16s at him and told him if he screamed again we were going to blow him away and that everyone here would swear that the V. C. killed him. We told him to get down now. This is your last warning, and everyone clicked the safety off. When he saw the look on our faces and the sound of the safety clicking off he decided that if he wanted to live he better get off. When he got off the tracks quickly left and we moved to our staging area and got in the staging circle. At dusk, we moved into our ambush site and set up for the night. We were all very scared so we stayed at 100% alert all night. We never saw any movement all night long so at about 8:00 a.m. we took up our claymores and cautiously worked our way back to the logger site. The squad leader went straight to the captain and told him what had happened with the guy from Chicago. In about 20 minutes a Huey helicopter arrived and three military policemen got off. They arrested the guy and took him to Long Binh Jail. He got to go where he wanted to. We found out later that he got six months of hard labor and a dishonorable discharge from the Army for cowardness. But he didn't care, he got out of the field alive and got to go home alive.

The Dog, we pulled into a small new firebase in the Northwest part of the Iron Triangle. The base consisted of six 155MM cannons. The engineers came in by helicopter two days prior and created a clearing for the new firebase. They didn't make much of a berm around it, but they encircled the base with three rolls of concertina wire that had one roll stacked on top of the other two.

It was unusual, but several young Vietnamese boys were hanging around outside the wire. They looked like they were teenagers. Our second platoon had somehow picked up a small stray dog and was hiding him out from their platoon leader. We had been told that were not to have any mascots. One of the 2nd platoon guys had the dog out of their track and the Lieutenant happened to walk by and see the dog. He went up to the grunt and started chewing him out about having any mascots. He tried to catch the dog, but the dog ran over by the wire. He walked up to the dog and pulled out his 45-caliber pistol and shot the dog dead. He then picked up the dog and threw it over the wire where the Vietnamese boys were. One of the boys was a head taller than the others and he got to the dog first. To the Vietnamese, out in the country dog meat was the number one chop-chop. Seven of the others jumped on the one with the dog. I had never seen such a kick fight. Some would get behind the big boy and kick him in the back of the head while he was taking care of the others in front of him. It went on for about fifteen minutes, and all of the boys were bleeding from their noses, lips, and ears. The big one with the dog finally won the fight against the seven others, and he walked off proudly with his prize.

The Canteen, as hot as it was in Vietnam you had to drink a lot of water to stay hydrated. We had plastic water bladder canteens and regular-sized plastic canteens. In the heat, the plastic canteen would take on a terrible plastic taste.

One of the ambushes that we blew as we were checking the dead bodies of the VC I noticed that one had a new-looking aluminum canteen on his belt. I had seen them on dead VC before but the thought never occurred to me that water would taste much better out of them. I took the new looking one off of the dead VC and put it on my belt on my web gear. When we got back to our logger site I rinsed the canteen out and filled it with water. It tasted much better than water out of our plastic ones. I carried the aluminum canteen for the rest of the time that I was in the field. I took it home with me and it is one of the two souvenirs that I have from Vietnam. The other thing is a bean flip that I took off of another dead VC

The Snipers Bullet, one day when I was acting platoon leader we were on a search and destroy mounted mission southwest of Cu Chi. We had checked out some of the areas that we were supposed to and were headed to our next objective. We came upon an area that didn't look right on my navigation map, so I told the tracks to stop. We stopped in a clearing with a wood line about 200 meters ahead of us. I had the squad leaders come to my track to look at the map with me to try to figure out which direction we were supposed to go. The track engines were all still running while we gathered up right by the side of my track to study the map. All of a sudden a shot rang out and from the loud crack of it we could tell it was very close. We all hit the ground and I yelled at the tracks to open fire. All of the 50s and 60-cal opened upon the wood line for about a minute and I ordered a cease fire. We didn't receive any more fire so we all got up off of the ground. As we were looking around I looked at the side of my track that we were standing almost against and I saw a groove in the side of the track where the sniper's bullet had hit. He only missed us by about six inches. We were lucky that he wasn't a good shot. We assaulted the wood line with all tracks firing everything that we had. We dismounted and checked the area out, but we didn't find anyone or anything. He must have taken the shot and then ran.

Mosquitoes, the mosquitoes were very bad in Vietnam, especially during the rainy season. We had army-issued mosquito dope that we put on, but it only worked for a few minutes. When you came in as a new guy with your light-colored skin they would eat you alive. After you were there awhile and had received a good sun tan they didn't bother you so bad. I remember my first night in the field I fought them as long as I could and I finally went to sleep. When I woke up my eyes, lips, nose, and ears had big bumps on them from all of the mosquito bites. There was a chance that you could catch Malaria from numerous mosquito bites, so we had to take two pills every day. I remember there was a small white one and a small pink one. I didn't know of anyone that came down with Malaria, so I guess the pills worked.

The 175 Fire Base, about three weeks before we invaded Cambodia our company was sent to secure another new firebase that was about five miles from the Cambodia border. The base had two 175-millimeter guns and eight 155-mm artillery tracks. We hadn't seen any big 175 artillery pieces before. I talked to the sergeant in charge of the 175 on my side of the site that was directly behind my track. He told me that the gun could fire the large projectile about 20 miles over into Cambodia and that the shell broke the sound barrier three times before it left its long barrel. He said that if they got a fire mission they would notify us so that we could get behind the big gun to avoid the huge concussion from the shell.

It was the first night for the firebase to be there so the Company Commander told us to be ready for mad minutes at any time during the night. We had set out three rows of claymore mines in front of our position, put up the RPG screen in front of the track, and dug an M60 machine gun fighting position on each side of the track.

Right after dark the CO called and said mad minute in zero one minute. I alerted everyone to get ready and the artillery sergeant behind us heard and came to me and asked if he could fire with us and throw a hand grenade. I told him sure but be sure and get the grenade out about 20 meters because we had a row of claymores just in front of the berm right in front of the tracks. When the mad minute started the artillery sergeant was standing on the berm to the side and front of my track. As we were firing everything I could see him in the muzzle flashes get a hand grenade and pull the pin on it. Just as he was getting ready to throw it he dropped it. I heard the pin pop as he was trying to pick it up. When he picked it up he just dropped it over the berm and hit the ground. When his grenade went off it set off all of the claymores that were in front of my track. When the mad minute was over I went to find him. When I found him I chewed him out for dropping the grenade and setting off our claymores and almost getting some of my guys killed.

I took the first duty behind the 50-cal gun that night I didn't see or hear anything for my hour of watch. I woke up Private Todd to replace me on guard. We had a hammock inside the track and when we were on bases the squad leader got to sleep in it. It was a hot night and the top hatch was up and the back hatch was down, I had just gone to sleep in the hammock when all of a sudden a concussion hit me and knocked me out of the hammock. I hurt all over and thought that I was probably hit with shrapnel. Bits of tree limbs and clods of dirt were raining down on us. I yelled at Todd and asked him if he was all right. He yelled back, "I'm okay I think!" I thought that we had been hit by an 81MM mortar round. I said, where did it hit Gary? He said it didn't hit it was that dang gun. He said, "I thought they were supposed to warn us before they fired it, but they didn't."

I got up mad, and with my ears ringing very loud. I went looking for that sergeant. When I found him I grabbed him by his shirt and lifted him off of the ground. I told him that he had probably ruined all of our ears for life, and why didn't he warn us like he said that he would before they fired the gun right over our heads? He said that it was an emergency fire mission and that they didn't have time to warn us. I knew that he was lying and that he was just trying to get even with me for chewing him out about dropping the hand grenade. I shoved him to the ground and told him it better not happen again or me and my boys will come after you! They had two more fire missions that night and they gave us plenty of warning time to get behind the big gun this time.

Pond Tunnels, were many kinds of tunnels that we found and destroyed in our area of operation. But one kind that we found showed the ingenuity that the VC had. Sometimes we would be pursuing V. C. in a running firefight and they would just miraculously disappear. It was usually in an area of big craters that were partly filled with water because of the rainy season. We called the bomb craters from 750 and 500-pound bombs instant ponds.

It wasn't until the dry season that we figured out how we were losing contact with the enemy in areas of the bomb crater ponds. The V. C. would dig a tunnel in the base of the crater when they were dry. They would dig straight back and then up above to where the water line would be during the rainy season. Then they would dig out a room and make a small breathing hole up through the top with a long sharpened bamboo stick. It was just like a beaver logger. They would dive into the water and swim up the hidden tunnel and climb into the room about the water line. This is how they were amazingly disappearing from us when we were after them.

Letters and Calls, as in every war in the past most soldiers looked forward to receiving a letter from friends and loved ones. We were also that way. They kept you up on what had been happening at home and what they had been doing. Even though you were thousands of miles away letters gave you a connection of home and a more secure feeling.

My wife wrote me a letter nearly every day and kept me up on anything that had been happening at home and on the things that our daughter was learning and doing. My mother wrote me a letter about once a week and kept me up on what they had been doing and how the farm was getting along. My grandmother wrote me three or four letters during my year in Vietnam. All the ones who were writing me told me that they were praying for my safe return home. When I wrote letters I couldn't tell where we were or what we had been doing. So I would just tell them about the weather and stuff like that. I got a letter from my mother and she wrote that my grandad

Whalen had passed away. I knew of a couple of guys that got to go home on emergency leave because of the death of a close relative.

I went to the captain and told him that I would like to put in for an emergency leave to attend the funeral of my grandfather. He told me that he was sorry, but he couldn't let me go because he needed his good leaders, and that I was one of them. So I didn't get the emergency leave. I got to call home twice while I was in Vietnam. We were in Cu Chi both times. The only way that we could call home then was by two-way radio. I called my wife both times and one of the times I got to tell her when my R&R was going to be and for her to make plans to meet me in Hawaii. When you were talking to your wife or girlfriend after every statement you had to say "over" and they had to do the same thing. Someone had to be listening to everything that was said and would change the radio over every time you said "over" It was like talking on a PRICK25 radio out in the field.

CHAPTER 46

New Area of Operations
Powered CS Gas

W e had been working in the Southeast sector of the Iron Triangle for about three weeks when we got a call that we were to move our area of operations to the Northwest sector of the Iron Triangle. We saddled up and rolled to our new area. It took us about four hours to get there. It was the dry season and by the time we arrived in our new area, we were covered by a thick layer of dust from the tracks in front of us. We all looked like DIRTMEN.

We met up with some units of Charlie Company and they told us that they had lost five guys the day before to a booby-trapped dud 500-pound bomb. They said that the Viet Cong had booby-trapped it with a vibration detection device. If a track got close to the bomb the vibration from the track would set off the bomb.

In the area that we had just left, we found several dud bombs and we used shaped charges that we made out of C-4 explosives to destroy them. We hadn't heard of the vibration detection devices with dud bombs before, but we always destroyed the ones that we found. We would find dud bombs that had been opened up and all of the explosives had been removed. The VC and NVA would use the explosives to make mackerel can booby traps. After they ate the fish they would take the cans and glue nails, bolts, bullet hulls, or any kind of metal that they could find to the inside of the can. Then they would fill it with explosives that they had removed from a dud bomb, put a percussion detonation device on top, and then melted wax on top with a paraffin wax seal. They would plant them in a trail or a rice patty dike and when someone stepped on it, it would explode. The mackerel can booby traps were the most common kind that we found and they were the main type of booby traps that our troops were wounded or killed by.

The new AO that we were now working on was quite a bit different than our previous areas. There were very few populated areas in it. There were no rice patties or crops that we could see. The area consisted of some jungle areas and old Rome plowed areas that had been sprayed with agent orange earlier and the brush was already coming back, and large cleared areas that were grown up with elephant grass. We figured that the elephant grass area was old rice patties that were not being used because of the war. The elephant grass was six or seven feet tall and very hard to walk through. There were also a lot of bomb craters in our new area.

It was very hot and we had to wear towels around our necks to keep the sweat out of our eyes. The mosquitoes in the area were really bad also, and we were reminded to be sure and take our daily Malaria pills. We had to take a little pink, and a little white pill every day to try to keep from getting Malaria.

When we started doing roving patrols in the area it didn't take us long to find out that there were lots of wait-a-minute vines in the area. If you ever walk into a wait-a-minute vine you will know why they were called that. The vines had claw-like hooked stickers on every branch and they definitely would stop you when one got a hold of you.

In the jungle part of our new A.O., there was an abundance of Red Ants. We had encountered red ants in the areas but not as many as we found there. Red ants are meat eaters. They hang in big globes up in the trees and if an animal or man walks under them the whole colony drops down on them and starts biting immediately with their big pinchers on their head. If red ants drop on you they would fall and crawl all down your shirt and pants and start biting you all over immediately.

We didn't wear shorts or socks out in the field because we were almost always soaking wet either with sweat or rain and you would get galled if your shorts and socks were always wet. If a colony of red ants came down on you it didn't matter who was around or what you were doing you would shuck your clothes as fast as you could because of the pain from all of the bites.

We were on a search and destroy mission one day and we would stay on the tracks from one place to the next. Every time we saw a hedge row or anything that didn't look right, we would dismount and check out the objective. We found many tunnels and spider holes in a lot of the hedgerows. We used Bangalore torpedoes to blow the tunnel systems up. We blew up several hedge row tunnel systems that day. As we were traveling to our next objective we had to drive through a large area of elephant grass. I was in the squad leader's seat on top of the track and one of my men was setting on the right front corner of the track and the rest of the squad was setting behind us on the APC. As we were driving across the area of elephant grass the tracks were scattered out on line about 40 meters apart. As we were driving through the elephant grass the right front corner of the track sharply dropped down as it hit a deep hole and the track suddenly tilted up. John Baumbtrong, a man in my squad, the one setting on the right front of my track fell off the track backward. I looked down at him and he was smiling because he thought that his fall was going to be cushioned by the tall thick grass. As I was watching him fall he and I both thought that he would stop falling when he got to the ground level, but he kept going down out of sight. I jumped off of the track and rushed over to him and he was lying in the bottom of a five-foot-deep pongee pit. In the earlier days of the Vietnam War, the Viet Cong dug lots of 5x5x5 deep pits and then put sharpened bamboo sticks all in the bottom of the pit. Then they covered the pit with small sticks, dirt, and grass. Anyone that fell in would be impaled on the sharp bamboo sticks. They would also put feces on the end of the sticks so that it would cause the victim to have serious infections.

John was lucky, when his back hit the pongee sticks the sticks were so old that they broke instead of puncturing him. I helped him out of the pit and he was no longer laughing as he realized what could have happened to him if the sticks hadn't broken. We backed the track up and continued our mission.

As we traveled to our next objective we came upon the place where the Charlie Company track had been blown up by a booby-trapped 500-pound bomb. It was a very sobering scene. The track was completely blown apart and the sides of the track were about 100 meters apart. I don't even know if there were any body parts left of the five guys on that track that were instantly killed. As we continued on our coordinates to our next objective we found a dud 250 bomb and another tunnel complex. We used a shaped charge to blow up the dud bomb and Bangalore to blow up the tunnel complex. As we were driving through an area that had about two-foot-tall grass I and everyone else was scanning the grass looking for dud bombs. We had gone about 150 meters through the area when I saw a dud 500 bomb about 10 meters in front of the track. I yelled at Rich Nichols, Back up, Back up, BOMB, BOMB. He immediately put the track in reverse and backed us up as fast as he could. Rich was my track driver and we called him Nick. We were all afraid that the bomb might be booby-trapped with a vibration device, but lucky for us it wasn't. After seeing the remains of the Charlie Company track blown away in every direction, we were very concerned that it could happen to us.

We would find a fairly open area every evening and set up a logger site. A Huey helicopter would fly out and bring us a resupply of food, ammo, and mail almost every other day. Each night we were sending out three eight-man ambushes. The first two nights none of the ambushes saw any enemy movement. On the third night, I took out one of the ambushes. My ambush didn't have any enemy movement, but the CO radio man called on the radio and told me that, White One, the 1st platoon's ambush had a positive situation and that they were getting ready to blow the ambush on a group of twelve VC soldiers. It was about 10:00 p.m. when we were called and they advised us to be on high alert for the next few hours. White One's ambush was about 500 meters to our Lima, which was the code word for the South for that day. I alerted everyone on my ambush to the situation and told them to be ready for anything from any direction but to especially watch to the South.

About three minutes later they blew the ambush with the claymore mines first then automatic weapons fire. I was listening to the PRICK25 radio as to what was going on and their RTO man said that they were receiving return fire from two different directions and that they had requested a helicopter gunship and artillery illumination. Before the helicopter arrived the parachute flare from the artillery popped over their location and lit up the area. They were still firing weapons, but the firing eased off when the illumination popped. The wind was blowing from them to us and as the flares were coming down they were coming down right on our position so I quickly passed the word for everyone to get as flat to the ground as possible, because we were going to be lit up like a Christmas tree. The helicopter arrived on the scene and made a few rocket and strafing runs and the firefight was over. We were lucky that no enemy was around us because the parachute flares all landed right next to us and we were lit up like a football field. The next morning while we were sweeping the area we found five Viet Cong that were KIA's and two blood trails leaving the area. We had no casualties.

We were on one of our afternoon searches and destroy missions when all of a sudden we hit strong CS gas. We had gas masks, but we usually just covered our mouths and nose with the sweat towel that we wore around our necks. We had hit the gas before, but this was the strongest we had hit with the tracks. It was an area that had been Rome plowed with giant D-12 bull-dozers, and the brush had been sprayed with Agent Orange defoliant to kill it. When these areas started growing back some of our helicopters would come in with fifty-gallon barrels of powdered CS gas and drop them around the area from a high altitude and they would hit the ground and splatter the powdered gas all over the area. When it would rain the gas would be imbedded in the soil and stay. Then if someone walked or drove across it the powdered gas would be stirred up and get you. They did the gas drops to try to prevent the Viet Cong and the North Vietnamese Army from regaining the area. We kept driving and finally made it out of the gas. We stopped and took turns pouring water into each other's eyes to stop the burning. It felt good to be able to see and breathe again.

We continued to our objectives to check out areas that may have enemy camps or arms caches in them. We came up on another area of elephant grass that was only about five feet tall. We were on a company size operation. The third platoon, my platoon, was the point platoon. All sixteen of our tracks were following in the single file and staying about forty meters apart. My track was the third track back from the point track. The point track was following a trail across the elephant grass, which we knew he shouldn't be doing. There was a tremendous explosion and the point track had hit a mine. It blew one idler wheel off of the track and broke a link in the right track. We watched the soldiers on top get blown about five feet up in the air and come down to the ground. When we hit a mine and got blown off it, we called it "airborne unqualified."

In my time in Vietnam, my track hit two mines and I went "airborne unqualified" twice. You go up like a rocket and it seems like you are floating down, that is until you hit the ground, and you soon realized that you weren't floating. After hitting a mine, it always took a couple of days for your ears to get where you could hear again.

The captain ordered all tracks to stop while he evaluated the situation. He asked the squad leader on the track that hit the mine if there were any causalities and if the track was fixable. The squad leader told him that everyone was okay except for the loud ringing in their ears and they thought that they could repair the track so that it could move. He told our platoon leaders to move our other three tracks forward and spread out to pull security for the track while they repaired it. Our platoon leader Lieutenant Smith instructed the drivers of the three tracks to stay off the trail and for the second two tracks to follow directly in the trail made by the lead track as we moved around the damaged APC to pull security for it.

My APC was the third track in line and Nick, my driver was trying to stay on the trail of the other tracks. All of us on top of the track started yelling at Nick telling him that he was to the left of the tracks. We were afraid that we would hit a mine if we weren't directly on the track of the other two APCs. I told him, "Let me drive this sucker," and he came out of the hatch and said, "There it is, you drive." I got in the hatch and started forward, I hadn't driven 20 meters until everyone started yelling, "You're off track, you're off track!" I stopped and one man in the squad said I can drive this machine and stay on track, so I said, "Have at it!" he revved up the engine and took off and almost immediately we all started yelling, "You're off track!" So he stopped, we all looked at each other, and in unison, we said, "Take it, Nick, we won't say anything." He was a good-natured guy and he said, "Anybody else wants to try it?" We all said "NO! You got it, Nick." In about 45 minutes, the squad of the damaged APC had it repaired and moved out to our next objective.

On the first three ambushes that I took out in the new A.O., we didn't make any contact with the enemy. But on the fourth one, it was a different story. We set up our ambush on the east side of the clearing that had short brush growing on it. There was a gradual slope downhill to our west. There was a heavy jungle with big trees all along the outside of the clearing. I had my men set out their clay-mores as far out as the detonation chord would reach because the trail that we were supposed to ambush ran along the outside of the heavy timber, and it was about 60 yards from us to the trail.

After setting out our claymores we settled in at 100% alert until 10:00 p.m. By 10:00 we hadn't had any enemy movement down the trail. We called in a negative site rep every hour. We were required when we were on an ambush to call in our situation either negative or positive. A positive meant that you had enemy movement in sight. I had found a two-foot tall berm which is where I set up the ambush so that if we did make contact with the enemy we would have some cover. We usually set up closer to the trail that we were supposed to ambush, but the berm was a good cover. It was a nice night, there was no wind and about ½ moon so the starlight scope worked very well.

After 10:00 p.m. we started our turns getting some sleep with one man at a time on guard duty. When you were on guard duty you would constantly scan the whole area around you with the starlight scope. After an uneventful night at 6:00 a.m. everyone was waking up and we were again on 100% alert. We usually stayed in an ambush until about 8:00 a.m. and then walked back to the company logger site. We hardly ever blew an ambush after it got light in the morning. So as we were about ready to take up the claymores and head back. I and the troop next to me saw seven VC come over the rise. They were coming down the trail that we were to ambush. We alerted the rest of the ambush members and everyone got ready. The VC was dressed in all-black pajamas and had cone-shaped hats on. It looked like they were all carrying AK47s. We all had the clackers to set off our claymore mines in our hands and we were about to blow the ambush with them when all of a sudden they turned and went into the wood line where we couldn't see them. We were whispering to each other wondering why they left the trail so abruptly. Did they see one of us?

About that time, they opened up on us and we were taking heavy AK fire from the wood line. We blew our claymores and started returning fire. I knew that we were probably going to have to have some help because we were taking fire from two directions. I got on the radio and requested immediate gunship help if anyone was in the area. I immediately got an answer from a Cobra helicopter pilot. He said his call sign was Dragon 1 and that he already had my ambush position on his map and that he and a little loach helicopter were on a hunter-killer team mission and that he was only about 12 to 15 minutes away. He said, "I am on the way." I said, "Roger that Dragon 1, this is White 3 and I appreciate your help."

The firefight was still going on after about 10 minutes. Our grenade launcher man, and M60 machine gunner were laying down heavy fire as were the rest of us with our M16's. we could hear the helicopters coming in the distance and we knew that he was only 2 or 3 minutes out. Usually, the V. C. would break fire and leave before the gunships arrived, but these didn't quit. We were still receiving fire when Dragon 1 arrived. Luckily, none of us had been killed or wounded as the berm was giving us good cover. You could hear the rounds hitting the berm in front of us and hear them cracking overhead, and the constant akk-akk-akk from all of the AKs. I got on the radio with Dragon 1 and told him that I had a visual of him. He answered White 3 this is Dragon 1 pop a smoke so that I can identify your position. I said, "Roger that, popping now." He immediately answered I have two yellow and one red smoke, looks like Charlie is listening to our radio. I immediately popped a green smoke and he said, "I have green." I answered that is us. I told him that we were still receiving fire from the wood line to our Romeo, which was a code word for the west that day. He answered, "Roger that, got the wood line, going to light them up."

He came in on a dive run down the inside edge of the wood line. He was firing rockets M60 min-gun, and automatic grenade launcher rounds. When a Cobra helicopter comes in on a dive fire run, it looks like an angry hornet coming at you. After his first pass, I told him that we were still receiving some fire from the wood line in the area that he hadn't fired at. He answered, "White 3, got it, I'll light the area up." He made the second pass with everything that he had and we stopped receiving fire. I told him, "Good job, Dragon 1 we appreciate your help." He answered, "Good luck White 3, getting low on fuel, going to return to base, out."

After things settled down the company commander was on the radio and asked me if we had any casualties. I told him no friendly ones, but probably some enemies were killed or wounded. He told me to be careful but to go check for bodies and keep a count. Body count seemed to be important to the officers at that time. We waited a few minutes and I told my men that we were going to check for bodies, but be ready to hit the ground if we start taking fire because there could still be some enemy alive. We started walking slowly across the clearing and I took point. When we reached the wood line we found seven dead VC with the AK47s. when we checked them out we found out why they didn't break contact even when the Cobra arrived. They were all women! We had always heard that the women were vicious fighters and that they wouldn't quit until you killed them or they killed you. We checked inside the wood line and found two more VC and several blood trails. We gathered up all of the AKs and headed back to the company logger site.

★　　★　　★

CHAPTER 47
Private Brown & Specialist
Pachinski Shot

P rivate Brown was a good soldier in my third platoon. He was from Arkansas and he was fun to be around. I had taken out several ambushes that he was on and he had always done a good job if we made contact with the enemy. One night that I didn't have to take out an ambush Private Brown went on one with the second platoon squad leader. We were in an area where our eight-man ambushes had been making contact with small groups of Viet Cong soldiers on a fairly regular basis. I listened on the PRICK25 radio to all of the SIT-Rep reports during the night of all three ambushes. Those of us that didn't have to go on ambushes stayed in the logger site to secure the tracks and to be ready as a reactionary force if one of the ambushes got hit.

None of the three ambushes that night observed any enemy movement. About one hour after daylight they all packed up and headed back to the logger site. Brown was walking point. As he worked his way through the edge of an opening the V. C. opened up on him from his left side with AK fire. He dropped to the ground and returned fire, but as he was going down he was hit through both gluteus maximus muscles, in other words, through the butt! We immediately jumped in our tracks and went to help them. By the time we got there, they were not receiving any return fire. We still pulverized the wood line that the AK fire had come from. The squad leader had already called for a dust-off for Brown. The medic had bandaged him up as best as he could to try and control the bleeding. We moved out in a big circle and set up security for the landing spot for the dust off. Everyone was joking with Brown about getting hit in the behind, even though he was making some jokes about it, but we knew that he was seriously wounded and needed to get to the doctor as soon as possible.

We called on the radio the next evening to check on him and we were told that he was recovering, but that his recovery would be a long one. We all thought that he would probably get to go home because of the severity of his wounds, but a month later the doctors released him back for duty. He was lucky that the Jeep, truck driver position in the rear area came open and he was assigned that job.

When I became the noncommissioned officer in charge of the rear area he was my Jeep, truck driver and he was my friend. He had been promoted to Specialist Fourth Class after he had recovered from his wounds.

Specialist Pachinski's story was very similar to Specialist Brown's. He was a member of my platoon and a third squad member. He had been with us for about five months and had proven himself to be very dependable in every situation that we encountered. It was another night that was my night off from taking out another ambush. It was the same as the ambushes three nights before. None of the three ambushes had observed any movement and when the third squad ambush patrol started back in, they got fired at the same as the Brown ambush did. Almost the same thing happened. Specialist Pachinski got hit from the side and took an AK round through both sides of his behind. We got to the site of the ambush as quickly as we could and fired into the wood line as we had done before.

Pachinski was hit even worse than Specialist Brown was and the medics were having trouble controlling the bleeding. The dust off chopper arrived shortly after the company did and Pachinski lost consciousness just before it got there. The medics were putting as much direct pressure on his wounds as they could, but the bleeding was still pretty bad. No one laughed or joked about his wounds because of the severity of them. We loaded him onto a stretcher and quickly put him on the dust-off. The medics started an IV as soon as they could and the chopper lifted off. We were still afraid that he wasn't going to make it because of the loss of so much blood. We checked on him the next day and the nurses told us that he had been stabilized in critical condition and then he had been flown out to a hospital ship for more specialized treatment. We were hoping that he would be alright and that he would recover from his wounds.

About a month later I received a letter from him. He said that he had been in a hospital for weeks and had to have several operations before he recovered from his wounds. He wrote that he was released from the Army because of combat disability wounds, that he was home back in the world, and that he was enjoying it very much. He wrote, I think of you guys every day and I pray that all of you get out of the Nam alive and well. Please give all of the platoon members my regards. We were all glad for him that he had survived his serious wounds and was now back in the world!

CHAPTER 48
River Patrol Boats Ambushes

We never knew what to expect every day in the mechanized infantry in Vietnam and Cambodia. We might be in the far north of our area of operation one day and then the next we have to saddle up and travel twenty-five or thirty clicks to a new area where intelligence determined that we were needed. The purpose of having mechanized infantry was to be able to move troops fast to a fight. Each day in the infantry in Vietnam and Cambodia was a movie.

One day we received orders to go southwest to an area that was several miles from our area of operations at the time. The area was a heavy jungle, swamp, and numerous rivers. When we arrived at the river the Company Commander called all platoon sergeants and platoon leaders to his track for a meeting. He told us that a company of straight-leg infantry had been ambushes in the area and that they had taken heavy casualties. He told me that he was sending the third platoon on three ambushes of trails in the area where the attack of the straight legs occurred. The second platoon was to do the same up river and I was supposed to go down river. The rest of the company would stay at the logger site to protect the tracks. He told us that we would be boarding RAG boats to take us close to our ambush sites. RAG stood for Riverine Assault Group watercraft. Before he released us from the briefing he told us that the ambushes would be for the rest of the day and all night. He informed us that the RAG boats would drop us off about two hundred meters from the trails that we were supposed to ambush and that they would extract us at 9:00 a.m. the next day. He told us that there will be three boats for each platoon's ambushes. Each eight-man ambush would get on a different boat. Then he told us that the boats would be here in thirty minutes to pick up all of the ambushes. Then the CO released us and told us to hurry and get ready, and "Good Hunting."

I told my guys this could be a bad area so pack all of the ammunition you can carry, water, and two boxes of C-rations. The river that we were on ranged from about one hundred and fifty to two hundred meters wide. We were ready to go, standing on the river bank when we heard the boats coming. When the boats pulled up to the bank we met crews of the three boats that were to take us downriver to our ambush sites.

The soldiers on the Riverine Patrol Boats were all wearing cut-off fatigue pants and no shirt or boots. We wondered how they got by with that, but we soon learned. They were all eighteen and nineteen years old draftees, and we learned that the life expectance of a RAG boat crew member was two to three months. That explained why the crew soldiers acted carefree and kinda crazy. It was probably the only way that they could face it. Running up and down the rivers without any shields on their weapons or anything to hide behind had to be extremely dangerous. Each RAG boat had a crew of five troops. If they got hit the only thing that they had to hide behind was the firepower that they put out.

We loaded onto the patrol boats and the boats blasted off downriver. As we set on the deck of the RAG boats while running down the river we could see some hooches along the banks every once in a while and the people would come out and watch us go by. The guys on the boat told us that some of the people were VC soldiers or sympathizers and that they would notify VC soldiers by radio that we were coming downriver. I could see why their life on the boats was so dangerous. All that they had in their favor to keep them alive when they were ambushed was the speed of their boats and their weapons. The areas that we passed looked like very dangerous places.

We arrived at our drop-off points without any trouble. We dropped off the second squad ambush first and then the first squad ambush. My third squad ambush was dropped off last. The trails that we were supposed to ambush were marked on our maps. All three ambushes would be about one-half mile apart. We quickly got organized and moved out. I used my compass to navigate through the jungle for about two hundred meters and then we hit the trail that we were supposed to ambush. There were numerous man tracks in the trail and it looked like it had been heavily used. We moved about one hundred meters up the trail and started setting up our ambush as silently as we could. We camouflaged ourselves as best we could and started the long wait.

About one hour before dark I passed the word for every other man to eat his C-rations while the other one kept watching for him, and then trade so the one that ate first watched for him while he ate. The heat and mosquitoes were very bad and only got worse as the night began to fall. We stayed at 100% alert until midnight and then I had two guys stay awake while the others slept. Every two hours we changed so that everyone would have a chance to try and get a little sleep.

The night went by without us encountering any enemy movement. The morning came and we were saddling up to go back to the river to be picked up by the boats. We were supposed to meet the boats one hundred meters upriver from where they had dropped us off so that the VC could not as likely ambush us. We were almost back to the river when heavy gunfire erupted upriver from us. My radio man told me that the second squad ambush was ambushed on their way back to the river. I spoke to the CO over the radio and he told me that the boats to pick us up would be there soon and that we were to go help the second squad. The first squad was to be taken upriver above the second squad and my squad was to be dropped off downstream from them. We were both to work our way to the second squad positions from both directions. Hopefully, we could trap some of the enemies between us. When we got off of the boats we could hear AK, M16, and M60 machine gun fire coming from upriver. It sounded like it was about two hundred meters from us.

We cautiously started working our way up a trail toward the gunfire. As we were getting fairly close we had bullets start hitting the trees all around us. I told my men to take cover behind trees and that the rounds were probably from our men. We were on the ground and behind trees to try to keep from being hit. Everyone was ready for anything and was watching the trail. There was a curve in the trail about twenty-five meters from us. Five VC soldiers came around the curve in the trail walking fast. They didn't see us. We were all so ready expecting anything that as soon as they appeared we all opened up at once with our M16s and ripped them up. After a short while the firing upstream ceased so we moved up to check the bodies and take their AKs. Then I had my men move up the trail about fifty meters and set up a quick ambush in case any more enemies came down the trail.

After a while after no more enemies showed up we slowly moved up the trail and were close to the second squad's position. I had my radio man tell them that we were coming in and for them not to fire downriver. When we arrived at the scene the first squad ambush had got there just ahead of us. Several dead VC were lying around the area. The first squad had the same story that we did. They were on the ground because of the firing. And seven VC came up the trail and they killed them all. The point man for the second squad's ambush was instantly killed when they were ambushed and the soldier behind him was hit in his left leg with a pretty severe wound.

While the medic was tending to the wounded man I had all of the rest of the men in the platoon space out evenly in a circle about 25 meters out for security for the wounded man. The Company Commander had already called for a dust-off chopper and he told me that it should arrive in about ten minutes. He ordered me to secure the area around the wounded man because the chopper would have to hover while lowering a drop basket through the trees because there was no clearing close enough to land in. I told him that I had already set up security and that we were ready. I did have everyone pulling security move twenty meters further out and take positions to be sure that the VC didn't get close enough to the helicopter to fire an RPG at it.

The dust off arrived and dropped the basket. We secured the wounded man on first and they winched him up through the trees. Then they dropped the basket down again with a body bag and zipped it up, and then secured it to the basket. As soon as the basket was pulled in the door the dust off chopper took off as fast as they could. The riverboats had been circling out in the river while firing their guns at the other side of the river just in case there were VC on that side that might try to fire at us.

I called them on the PRICK25 radio and told them that we were ready to be picked up. They answered we'll be there shortly. They picked us up and then headed back upriver. We arrived at our logger site without any trouble. The captain sent out three ambushes that night to help secure the tracks and the logger site. The next day was a repeat of the day before for my third platoon. The only difference was that we went upriver instead of down. The boats dropped us off without any trouble. We moved to our separate ambush locations and set up for the afternoon and night.

The time went by slowly because every man was apprehensive because of what happened the day before. We were pretty sure that we would probably make contact with Victor Charlie this time.

Morning finally came and none of the three ambushes had seen any enemy movement. Before 9:00 a.m. we picked everything up and headed back to the extraction site on the river. We were very careful on our way to the pickup site because of the ambush the day before of the second squad's ambush patrol as they were working their way back to the river. We got to the pickup site just as the River Boats came into view. We quickly piled on the boats and headed back.

We were about one-half way back to our logger site when we started taking AK fire from the north bank of the river. The river at the point was only about 150 meters wide and we were out in the middle. The crew of the river assault boat jumped on their weapons and started firing at the north bank while screaming like Comanche in a Western movie. They fired their M60 machine guns, 50-cal machine guns, and their twin 20-millimeter Ack Ack guns as fast as possible. My squad and I lay flat on the deck and fired our weapons as fast as we could. Since we didn't have any cover, fire superiority was the only chance that we had to survive. The boat driver pushed the throttle down to full throttle and started swerving back and forth to try to get us out of there as soon as he could. We could hear rounds cracking overhead and heard some hit the hull of the boat. It was a short firefight because the river patrol boats had powerful engines and the drivers got us out of there fast.

Luckily no one was hit. After that encounter, we had even more respect for the soldiers that had to be on those RAG boats Riverine Assault Crafts. They told us that they got hit about two or three times a week as they patrolled up and down the rivers. We arrived back at the logger site and the Company Commander notified me on the radio that we were ordered to go back to our old area of operations.

While riding on my track on the way back I thought, I've seen two jobs that I wouldn't want to trade places with. One was a heli-copter door gunner on a Huey or Loach helicopter, and the other was a soldier on a RAG patrol boat. We had great respect for the guys that performed these jobs.

CHAPTER 49
NCOIC

The job of sergeant in charge of the rear area came open and the captain picked me for the job. I had a little less than six weeks to go on my tour of duty and that probably saved my life by not being in combat anymore. In the rear area, there were four people assigned. First Sergeant Tinga, Clerk Typist Private Bernard, truck, and jeep driver Specialist John Brown, and NCOIC me, Sergeant E-5. My job was to process in and out those coming into the country and those going home or going on R & R. I had to make sure everyone was signed up correctly for their flights to and from their destinations. I had to send the new troops to a two-day in-country refresher course before I sent them out in the field. I had to be sure that resupply choppers got everything out to the troops. Their mail, chow, C-rations, ammunition, water bladders, one case of warm beer per squad once a week, and anything else that was requisitioned was part of my job to see that it was delivered.

Also, it was my job to see that anyone that came in on sick call got to the doctor and if they were on profile to keep them in the barracks until they were released by the doctor and then send them back to the field. The hardest part of my job was to meet the wounded at the hospital when the dust-offs brought them in and to go to the morgue and help make an identification of the KIA. I also had to see that any training needed in the field to meet regulations was taken care of and to keep a record of them.

First Sergeant Tinga, John Brown, and I would set around the radio every night and listen to the situation reports of our ambushes that night. If an ambush was blown, we would wait to see if anyone was wounded or KIA. if a dust off was called in John and I would go to meet the chopper to console the wounded and just be there so they know that someone was watching out for them. Lots of the time the doctors and nurses were so busy they couldn't keep constant watch over all the wounded.

I was in my little office one day and John Brown was there with me. My office was only a ten-foot by ten-foot section of the building up front by the first Sergeants Office. It had plywood walls that were open at the top with no ceiling, and there was only one door. John was setting in a chair and leaning back against the wall when an Arvin Soldier that had a big pet boa snake wrapped around his neck stepped into the door and said, "See snake." I don't think I have ever heard such a yell. John jumped up and climbed the wall and went over the top spouting various bad words. I didn't know that he was so afraid of snakes. He was worse than anyone that I had ever seen.

An idea came to me that could help solve a problem. Nearly every night John had been going to the enlisted man's club and getting fairly drunk and then he would come back to the barracks, turn on the light and start waking everyone up yelling and shaking bunks. Every day when we got out of our bunks we were to "S" roll the mattress. I thought that would be a fine place to put the snake, "In his bunk." I talked to the Arvin Soldier and ask him about his pet. He told me that he only fed it once or twice a year and that he would give it a whole live chicken. I asked him if he would stay if he was put on an "S" rolled mattress. He said, "Yes," he is very docile and will stay anywhere you put him if it is kind of dark. It sounded good to me so I asked him if I could keep him until morning and why. He smiled and said, "Okay." We went to John's bunk and put the snake inside his "S" rolled mattress and left him there. John's bunk was next to mine, so I would be close to the action. Everyone who was there knew what was going to happen. We turned the lights out and no one went to sleep because they didn't want to miss the action. About 11:00 p.m. we heard him coming. He was singing real loud when he came busting through the screen door. Everyone was acting like they were asleep. He shook a few bunks and tried to wake a few up then he finally gave up because he couldn't get a response from anyone. He came over to his bunk and he was singing real loud. I had one eye open and I was watching him when he jerked the mattress open. There was a brief silence and then a blood-curdling scream and he ran so hard into the screen door that instead of opening like normal it came off of the hinges and opened long ways. He was yelling as he went out, "Give me an M16, give me an M16!" The owner of the snake came by the next morning and got his snake. He asked me what happened. I told him and he and his pet left with him laughing.

One night when I was NCOIC, First Sergeant Tinga had gone to bed and John Brown and the Clerk Typist had gone to the enlisted man's club to get a drink and I was by myself listening to the Sit-Rep report on the radio. Right before dark a call went out from the 3rd platoon for two dust offs. I didn't know what had happened and I waited a while to see if I could hear any more information. After a while, I thought that I would go to the hospital and wait on the dust-offs to come in. I got in the jeep and drove myself to the hospital area. When I arrived the dust offs had already landed and the wounded had been taken to the first ward hospital. The Candy Striper at the desk told me that they had brought in six soldiers that were wounded. When I walked in the door of ward one I could see five of them were lined up on beds. One was at the back of the room and four doctors and one nurse were working on the sixth soldier. He was having a seizure because of wounds to the head and they were trying to stabilize him so that he could be flown out to a hospital ship where more care was available. I went down the line checking on all of the wounded and talked to each one and asked them how they were doing. The first soldier that I talked to told me what had happened. He said that the new sergeant E-6 had parked his track in the kill zone of a mechanical ambush with the whole squad setting on top of the track and that when the sergeant had hooked the PRICK25 battery to the mechanical it went off, and sprayed everyone on top of the track with pellets. He said that the new sergeant had made a bad mistake. I asked him where he was hit, the bandages that the medics had put on were on the calf of his left leg and one on his left forearm.

Then I went to the next man. The second one that I talked to was a young private that I had sent out only about three weeks before. We had found out from him that he was only seventeen years old and that he had got his mother to sign that he was eighteen years old so that he could get into the army. I asked him how he was doing and he said, "All right sergeant." I asked him where he was hit and he told me that, he got two of them, one in the ankle and one in the side. I asked him are you sure you are all right, and he said, "Yeah, I'm all right." I went to the next and he showed me his left ankle where he had been hit by one of the projectiles. He said that he was making it fine and that the medics had given him and the others morphine for pain. The next soldier in line in the row of beds was hit in the left thigh and calf by two balls from the claymores, and he said that he was doing fine.

As I started to go to the next man I saw that the doctors were still trying to stabilize the man with the seizures. He had been hit by four balls in his head and two in his arms. Just as I got to the last man I turned to look back at the others. I saw that the young kid didn't look good. I could see the color leaving his face rapidly. I asked him, are you okay? He weakly said, sergeant I don't feel so good. I could tell that something was bad wrong so I turned to the doctors and yelled, somebody come and check this man. Two doctors turned and looked at me. I had already gone back to the boys bed, and one doctor dropped what he was doing and told one of the other doctors to take over. He rushed over to the boys bed and immediately started yelling orders to the nurse to bring him several items as fast as possible. The nurse came quickly with a scalpel, a pint of alcohol, a pint of methylate, some gauze and gave them to the doctor. Then the nurse quickly brought a big glass water bottle and a piece of rubber tubing with a glass tube on the end of it. The glass tubing was angled on the end of it. The doctor took the bottle of alcohol and just splashed it on the side wound and then poured the bottle of methylate on it. Then he grabbed the scalpel and told the soldier, "This is going to hurt, son." I was standing right by the doctor as he slashed a cut between two ribs and then jammed the glass tube into his chest cavity. I can still remember the scream that the boy let out when that happened. There was so much pressure that had built up in him that when the tube was inserted it was so high that the tube that was in the big glass jar came out of the bottle and blood shot all the way across the room and ran down the wall. The nurse caught the tubing and put it back in the jar. The doctor called assistance and one of the other doctors came to help him. They gave him ether to quickly put him out and started operating on him immediately. I had seen a lot of bad stuff in Vietnam, but the blood shooting across the room and running down the wall, caught me by surprise and it made me feel woozy. I had to put my head down to keep from fainting.

I watched the whole operation. They went in and clamped off an artery that was damaged by the steel ball and had broken open. As they were completing the stitching part of the operation I asked the doctor why he had to immediately open the chest cavity up. He told me that the pressure of the blood buildup in the chest cavity can cause the heart to stop beating, and I think that it was about to happen. They put an IV in one arm of the young soldier and were giving him blood transfusion in the other arm.

While the operation was going on I saw the medics and other doctors take the soldier with severe head wounds out to be put on a chopper to be flown out to a hospital ship neuro specialist surgeon. After he was gone the other doctors started treating the other wounded men. I stayed until they all had been cared for and until the young kid with the punctured artery woke up from the sedative. The doctor told me that he believed that all of the soldiers that were still in the hospital would recover from their wounds. He told me that if I hadn't seen the soldier losing his color and told them to come and look at him, that he wouldn't have lasted for five more minutes. So I was really glad that I went to meet the wounded guys that night. I never did hear anything about the man that was hit in the head. I just hoped that he made it. The rest of the soldiers all gradually recovered from their wounds and returned to duty with Bravo Company.

One day when the resupply chopper come in there were seven black soldiers that came in for sick call. I had John drive them to the doctor's office and stay with them until they all saw the doctor. The back of their hands and elbows were all swollen. The doctors couldn't figure out what was wrong with them so they were put on permanent profile and staying in the rear area until the doctors could determine what was causing the swelling. They had been in the rear for about a week when Specialist 4th Class Tilley, a black soldier that had been in my platoon came in to go home. Tilley I think was from Southern Georgia, and he was a very good soldier. I told him about the seven guys that were in on profile with swelling and he said, "Sergeant Whalen, don't you know what them bloods are doing?" I told him no, that I had no idea. He said, "I've seen them do it, they have needles and they are shooting cigarette lighter fluid into the back of their hands and elbows to try to get out of the field." I thanked him and wished him well on his way home, and then I went straight to First

Sergeant Tinga and told him what Specialist Tilley had told me. He called the MPs and they showed up and arrested all of them. I don't know what happened to them because we never saw them again.

One night Specialist Brown and Private Bernard the Company Clerk Typist came back from the club together. They were both pretty well-lit. Bernard was a small framed guy and he had said at one-time that he was a gymnast in high school. Private Bernard was very quiet and usually didn't talk much, but John had him going. John was having him do stuff and he wanted everyone to watch. Bernard was doing standing back flips and then falling down and then John had him walk on his hands from one end of the barracks to the other. I told them to quit and that someone was going to get hurt, but they didn't, and sure enough Bernard tried to do a flip out of his hand walking. When he came up he fell on the steel corner of the bunk and cut a gash out about one-inch long over his eyebrow above his right eye. I had a guy get some bandages and I held pressure on it until the bleeding almost stopped. I got a good look at it and told him you need to get some stitches in it. He was still drunk but calm and he said, okay. The infirmary was about 100-yards from our barracks so I held his arm and walked him over to be sewed up. When I got him to the infirmary the doctors had him lie down on an operating table and one doctor looked at the cut and told him, "Yeah, you need some stitches in that, son." They cleaned the cutoff and started towards him with the needle to numb the area. When he saw the needle he started kicking and screaming, "I'm going to get killed in Vietnam!" over and over. Then he jumped off the table and ran out the door. I told the doctors, I'll get him back. I caught up with him and calmed him down and he agreed to go back in and have the cut sown up. He got back on the table, and exactly the same thing happened when they started towards him with the numbing needle. I retrieved him again and the doctors told him that this was the last time that they were going to try to sow him up. Again he said, "Okay." And then the same thing happened again, only this time he kicked one doctor in the stomach and hit the other one with his elbow. Then he ran out the door again crying, "I'm going to get killed in Vietnam" when I caught him he kept saying that and I told him, yea that type writer is likely to get you. He jerked loose from me and started running again, and he ran off the edge of a four-foot drainage ditch. I got him out of the ditch by his collar and he was all muddy from the mud in the ditch. He started fighting me so I hit him with a hay maker swing and knocked him out, then I drug him back to the infirmary and threw him on the table, then I told the doctors to sew him up now you won't need anything to numb it with. They gave him the stitches that he needed and he came to. I walked him back to the hooch and put him to bed. The next day he was back to his usual quite self and he never mentioned the night before.

First Sergeant Tinga and I were listening to the radio one day and the Company Commander called in a dust off and we knew someone was hurt. That was all the information that we had that evening. The next morning one of my platoon members came in on the resupply chopper to go on R & R and he told us that Private Thornton had stepped on a booby trap and was hurt badly. So, he and John Brown, and I decided that we needed to go see him and check out how he was doing. When we got to the hospital we stopped at the front desk of the first building and asked a Candy Striper who was working the desk what ward that Private Thornton was in. She said, Ward B. I asked her where Ward B was located and she said that it was at the far end of the row of quasit huts. We thanked her and went to find Ward B. We had no idea what we were going to see in Ward B. We just opened the door and walked in. That ward was just a long open room with about fifteen beds on each side of the middle aisle. We froze in place at the sight of what we saw! Every bed had a wounded man that had lost at least one limb. Most of the severely wounded had lost two or more libs and four of them had no arms and no legs!

In the back of the room, four doctors were operating on a kid that had just been brought in shortly before we got there. The doctors just looked at us and never said a thing. They just went back to work. We whispered to each other, I don't know if we are supposed to be allowed to come in here or not. We slowly walked down the aisle looking for our friend, and we walked right by him and didn't recognize him because he had bandages on his head, and his left arm and left leg from his knee down were gone. We turned around and started walking back and he said, "Hi guys, come to see me?" We were embarrassed that we didn't recognize him on the way in, but we quietly talked to him for a while, and he told us, I'll be alright, at least I get to go home alive. We told him that we would be praying for him, and then we slowly left the building. The images that we saw that day will be burned in my mind forever.

The Preacher, one evening when I was making sure that everything needed was going out on the resupply helicopter, a new replacement troop walked into the office with First Sergeant Tinga and me. He was a good-looking black private and he introduced himself as a Preacher. He said that God had sent him there to kill communists and he wanted to get after it as soon as possible. I glanced at Top and he gave a "somethings not right here" look. I told the private that you have to go to the two-day in-country refresher course before being sent to the field. He answered, "I'm ready, put me out there now, I'm here to do God's work and kill communists." I told him that you do know that they kill back, don't you? He said, "The Lord will protect me, send me out now!" I looked at First Sergeant Tinga and I could tell that he was getting perturbed by the private. I said Top, what do you want to do with him? He answered, "If he wants to kill V. C., send his butt out on the resupply helicopter."

I gave John Brown his papers and told him to take the private to the chopper pad and put him on it. We were listening to the radio in Top's office and just as the resupply helicopter was landing the whole logger site got hit by a fairly large enemy force. The company was returning a heavy volume of fire and you could hear it on the radio. Squad leaders were directing fire to the areas that the fire was coming from. The resupply helicopter kicked out all of the supplies in the load while hovering and told the Preacher to jump off as they needed to get out quick because they were taking fire. He refused to jump to they pulled away as quick as possible taking him back with them.

First Sergeant Tinga had retired for a shower and to go to eat in the mess hall. John Brown and I were the only two left in the office. We were still listening to the firefight on the radio when the Private came busting into the room crying and screaming that he wanted to see a Chaplin! I said I thought that you were going to kill some V. C.? He said, "It's bad, it's bad, I want to see a Chaplin!" I don't know what happened to me, I guess built-up rage came out, but I started hitting him with my fists. I knocked him down and I was beating him with both fists.

Someone grabbed my arm and said stop! You're going to kill him. It was John, and he said to me, "He's not worth killing." I came to my senses and called the MPs and they came and picked him up. I don't know what happened to him. We never saw him again. I don't know how he made it through basic and advanced infantry training, but he did.

I had about three weeks to go when our company got hit while on a daytime search and destroy mission. Top and I were listening on the radio and it didn't sound good. They called for two dust-offs and said that they had four severely wounded and three with light wounds. Top and I jumped in the jeep and John Brown drove us to the hospital. They were already caring for the wounded seven when we arrived. We went in to check on them and they were getting ready to operate on the four severely wounded and we couldn't talk to them. We talked to the other three and they said that the whole company walked into an ambush, and to blow the ambush the V. C. had set off four or five DH-10s, which was the enemy's version of claymore mines. They said that most of the ones that were hit were from those command-detonated mines. They said that it was a pretty intense firefight and that it lasted until the company tracks got there and lit up the area with their 50-cal machine guns. They also said that two Cobra helicopters arrived just after the tracks arrived and that they sprayed the area that the enemy was in with mini-gun rounds and rockets. We asked one of the soldiers that we were talking to who the other four wounded were and he named three squad leaders and one platoon sergeant. We stayed with the troops until all of the operations and patching-up surgery were completed. The doctors told us that they thought that all of the wounded would survive. We returned to the headquarters area and started getting provisions ready for the evening resupply flight.

The next morning Top called me from his office and said, Sergeant Whalen comes in here, I need to see you. I reported to him and he told me that the Commander had called and that he had contacted the Battalion Headquarters and requested a replacement for the four Sergeants that were severely wounded, and that they had told him that none were available that they knew of, but that they would try to acquire some replacements as soon as possible. Then First Sergeant Tinga told me that the captain wanted me to get my stuff ready and that he may need me back in the field because of the loss of four leaders.

So I went back to my cot and packed my stuff in my duffle bag and got ready to go back out. I had an 8x10 picture of my wife and daughter and I got it out and stared at it for a long time. I remember thinking this may be the last time that I get to see an image of them. When I got the job as NCOIC I thought that since I had survived out in the field for several months and was then assigned to the rear area I had a good chance of getting out of Nam alive. But, now I wasn't so sure. I would have to lead men and face combat again. I was supposed to ride out to the company area that afternoon on the resupply chopper. I had my M16 and ammo and my duffle bag ready to go. Just as John Brown and I were about ready to go to the chopper pad, Top got a call from the captain and told him to tell Sergeant Whalen to stand down and that he was supposed to receive four NCO replacements. He also told Top to tell me to keep my stuff packed just in case he needed me. Lucky for me all of the replacements showed up and I didn't have to go back out in the field.

The Snake Bite, three evenings before I was to go home we were listening to the radio, and our company called for an extreme emergency dust off. We thought that someone had stepped on a booby trap and was wounded badly. John Brown and I met the chopper at the hospital and when they were unloading the private on a stretcher we could see that he was having seizures. We walked with the medics as they were taking him in and I asked, what is wrong with him? I don't see any wounds. One of the medics said, "Cobra snake bite!"

We found out later that our company was pulling security for a firebase that night and that the man that was bitten went down into a bunker and set down on some filled sandbags then reached around to lay something on a little shelf and the snake bit him on his left arm. They were doing all that they could for him, but we couldn't see any improvement in his condition. I called to check on him every day until I left Vietnam and he was still alive, but in a coma. As many poisonous snakes as there were in Vietnam, it is a wonder that a large number of soldiers weren't bitten. Nighttime ambushes and nighttime roving patrols I'm sure I came close to being bitten many times and didn't even know it.

One kid in my platoon liked snakes and he was always catching them and playing with them. Everyone would usually stay pretty clear of him when he had a snake in his hands. One day he had a small brown spotted snake in his hands and he brought it over to me to see it. I figured that it was a nonpoisonous snake and it seemed to be pretty tame, about that time our Chu Hoi scout Ringo walked over and when he saw the snake that the kid was holding I could see Ringo's face turning pale. He told the kid, "Throw away now, he bites you, you die!" The kid pitched the snake back in the brush and he was very lucky that he didn't receive a serious bite.

When we would blow up hedge rows of bamboo with tunnel systems under them, we would go in after the explosion to check things out. Every time we would find pieces of many different kinds of snakes. We even had a big cobra charge a track one day and the soldier behind the 50-cal blew him to pieces. Someone later told us that was what big cobras do when something invades their home area.

I had my duffle bag all packed and ready to go home with only two nights to go. I was busy in my office doing some paperwork and I looked at my watch it was a little past time for me to send everyone in the barracks to chow, so I stopped what I was doing and went to the barracks and told everyone to go to chow, they all left to go to the chow hall which was only about 90-meters away from the company area. I returned to my work and was trying to get it all completed. I was almost finished when I started hearing talk in the barracks. I looked at my watch and it was only nine minutes until the mess hall closed. I was hungry so I dropped what I was doing and hustled to the mess hall. The cooks were already cleaning up and getting ready to leave for the night. I asked if I was too late and one cook said no, I'll fix you a plate. When he brought me the plate I was the only one eating and some of the cooks were already leaving the building. Before I finished eating the last cook to leave came by and said, for me to just put the tray on the counter when I got through eating and they would wash it in the morning.

I finished eating and put my tray up and left the building and headed back to the company area. When I was a little over one-half the way back to the company area I heard a loud whoosh sound go over my head. I turned my head to follow the sound. It went all the way to the mess hall and hit with a tremendous explosion. I saw the mess hall completely obliterated! It was an indirect fire V-22 rocket that the V. C. had fired from a long distance away. If they would have fired it thirty minutes sooner when the mess hall was full, there would have been mass casualties. If they would have fired it five minutes sooner, I would have been the only one left in the building and obviously would have been killed.

I had one more day before I was to go home and I thought, *It ain't over until it's over.* A cold chill went down my spine when I realized how close I came to getting it again!

CHAPTER 50

The Death of Gary Todd

G ary Todd was a very likable guy that was assigned to my platoon while I was a platoon sergeant. He was a good soldier and always reacted well in a combat situation.

He was "Chosen To Serve" right after he graduated from high school. He told me that he had gotten married to his high school sweetheart before he had to leave for the Army. He was only eighteen years old. He had been there about five months when I was appointed sergeant in charge of the rear area.

After six months in Vietnam, a soldier could take a seven-day R & R leave, but the only places that you could go were Australia, Germany, Bancock Thailand, and Hawaii. Most married guys or guys with girlfriends would go to Hawaii and meet them there. Private Todd came into the rear area to process out for R & R about a month after I was NCOIC. I talked to him quite a bit as I processed him out. He was very excited that he was going to meet his new bride in Hawaii. He showed me a picture of her. She was a beautiful girl.

When he returned from R & R he came to me and said, "Can I talk to you, Sergeant Whalen?" I told him, any time you can talk to me. He said, "Sergeant Whalen, I have a bad feeling that I'm not going to make it out of here alive." He had tears in his eyes as he said that. I knew that it was tough leaving your wife and thinking that might be the last time she ever sees you. I had the same feeling when I left my wife in Hawaii. I tried to console him and give him confidence that he would make it. I told him, just take it a day at a time and be aware of his surroundings every second of the day. Be there with a clear mind.

About a week later First Sergeant Tinga and I were listening on the radio to the chatter about the operation that Bravo Company was carrying out that day. All of a sudden they called for a dust-off helicopter. They said that a soldier had stepped on a powerful booby trap and they needed help as soon as possible. Part of my job as a sergeant in charge was to meet the wounded at the hospital and to go to the morgue and positively identify the soldier or soldiers who were killed. When I arrived at the hospital and asked about the soldier from Bravo Company that just came in. I said, what ward is he in? The Candy Striper at the desk hesitated and said, "I'm sorry, he is not here, he is at the morgue." It hit me pretty hard because I was hoping that whoever it was would make it.

When I arrived at the morgue I told them that I was with Bravo Company of the 2nd of 22nd infantry and that I was there to give a positive identity of the deceased. When they opened the body bag I saw that it was Gary Todd. I almost broke down when I saw him. He was such a good man and a good soldier. I verified his identification and then slowly walked out. The thoughts that kept going through my mind were the same every time. We lost a good soldier and a good man. I hope what we are doing is worth this, "What a WASTE!"

CHAPTER 51

Jerry Calhoun
Going Home

When I had about two weeks to go on my tour in Vietnam, Jerry Calhoun, my best buddy, came into the rear area of Bravo Company to process out and go home. I was the sergeant in charge of the rear area so it was my job to process him out. He was to be discharged from the U.S. Army at this time because he had voluntarily extended his tour of duty in Vietnam for three months. When he got home he would be a Veteran Civilian.

After processing him out he was going to Tan Son Nhut Air Base to leave the next morning. I set up a ride on a Huey helicopter for him to get there the next morning. So he had to spend his last night in the screen barracks with me and the company rear area staff. He had never told me why he extended three more months in Vietnam so that he would be out of the Army when he got home. He said, let's go to the NCO club and I'll buy you a drink. I didn't drink much, but I said I'll go with you. He ordered two drinks for himself and one for me as I told him that I only wanted one. After drinking his two drinks he ordered another and then he started talking. He said, "I told you that I would tell you why I extended my stay here to get out of the Army and go home a civilian." He told me that about two months before he was drafted that he had gotten married to his high school sweetheart. He told me that his wife, mother, and sister had written him letters every day. After about seven months he said that he stopped receiving letters from his wife. He had written a return letter to all three every chance he got, and he thought something must be wrong. He said that he was still receiving letters from his mother and sister, so he wrote his sister and asked her to tell him what was going on. He said that he told her to not lie to him. In the second letter after that, she wrote him that she hated to tell him what was going on because of his situation, but that she would. She told him that his wife was running around with a guy that they were in high school with. He said after that I quit writing letters home and extended for three months.

When I took him to the chopper pad to catch his ride to the air base he said to me, "I'll write you after I get home and tell you what happened." He said, "I know your address." About a week later I received a letter from him. He wrote, "I told you that I would let you know what I did, so here it is. He said that when he got home, he didn't tell anyone that he was home. He wrote that there is a Dairy Queen in the area that he lived in and a lot of the young people gather there almost every night. He figured that his wife and her boyfriend would stop up there. He said that there was a two-story hotel across the street from the Dairy Queen and that he rented a second-story room that had a window where you would watch the Dairy Queen. He wrote that about five o'clock the first evening, they pulled up in her boyfriend's convertible. He said, "I diddy bopped down the stairs and across the street and walked up to her side of the car and leaned in the door and when she turned around he said, 'Hello Babe'." He wrote, "I wish you could have seen the look on her face." He said that he slapped her in the face! Her boyfriend got out of the car, and he said, "I preceded to knock many bumps on his head." I had heard of this happening to some troops in Vietnam, but I didn't think that it would happen to me. He said, what she did to me is about the lowest thing that a woman can do to a man! When a guy is in combat and far away and there is nothing that you can do it is a very helpless feeling. He said I'm getting rid of her. If you ever get a chance to come to Winston Salem look me up and we'll go have a good time and celebrate getting out of Vietnam alive. Good Luck, and hope you made it home safe your buddy, Jerry Calhoun.

CHAPTER 52

Leaving Vietnam

Finally, my markdown calendar was full and I had served all of my tour of duty in Vietnam. I shook hands with all the staff in the company area and said goodbye. Then I picked up my duffle bag and told my buddy John Brown, "Let's go, take me to the chopper pad."

As the chopper lifted off I waved goodbye to him. The chopper took me to the Tan Uyen airstrip where I was to board a plane to California. You always worried when you were in Tan Uyen because it wasn't the nickname "Rocket City" for nothing. They were hit at random times with the big V-22 rockets like the one that hit the mess hall. I wouldn't feel safe until our plane cleared Vietnam air space.

To check out they took all of the soldiers that were going home to a big room and told us that we would pass through another room before we were in the last room where we would be issued a new dress uniform and receive our orders to our next duty station. In the middle of the room, they told us that it was our last chance to legally get rid of any contraband. They instructed us that if we had any pictures of dead V. C. or any U.S.-made weapons we were to leave them on the table in the room. Also, the only weapons that we could take home were those not capable of fully automatic fire. SKS rifles and the P38 pistols were legal to take home. They said that our luggage would be checked at random in the next room and if you were found to have contraband instead of going home you would go to the Long Binh Jail.

I had my U.S. 1911 Colt 45-cal pistol that I took off an NVA officer, and that I had carried for most of the year with me. I debated in my mind if I should risk it or not. I grudgingly decided to leave it on the table in the room. But, when we went into the next room they were only checking about every 5th man and I went right through without being checked. I could have got it through, but it wasn't worth the risk.

We walked through the uniform line and they asked us our pant and shirt sizes and gave us uniforms that fit. They had a plastic bag with everything you needed to decorate your uniform. They had a packet with your name on it with the metals you had earned in it to also put on your uniform. There was a dressing room where we got our uniforms ready and then put them on. Also, new shoes were given to us. I left my jungle fatigues on the floor of the changing room.

After everyone that was going to be on our plane was ready they put us in formation and called out our names to come forward and receive our new orders for our next duty station. I opened mine and I was kind of shocked that it said, "Germany." I thought I have been away from my family for basically a year and a half and now I'm going to have to be away for another six months. After everyone had received their orders they marched us to our buses that took us to our plane. They put us in formation again and took our duffle bags to be stored on the plane and when they were loaded they formed us in a single line and we boarded the plane. There were a lot of smiles that you could see on a lot of the GI's faces.

Finally, the plane started moving and when the wheels left the runway it was a very good feeling. It didn't seem real. We had heard of planes being shot down before they left Vietnam air space and we couldn't relax until the pilot came on the speaker system. He announced gentlemen look out the window on the right side for the last look at Vietnam. A big cheer went up as the pilot dipped the wing several times so that everyone on the plane could see their last look. I noticed that the plane was full of cigarette smoke and you could hardly see the front of the plane. It was a big difference from the plane trip over where hardly anyone smoked.

Anyway, we were on our way home!

CHAPTER 53
U.S. Army

There were some things that I liked about the Army. In the enlisted ranks, if you did a good job, they would reward you with a job with more responsibility and usually an upgrade in rank. If you showed courage in combat, they would reward you with metals regardless of your skin color or where you came from. There didn't seem to be any politics involved in rewards or promotions for enlisted men. We had heard that in the officer's ranks that there was some politics involved in promotions, but we didn't know for sure.

If you did something above normal actions in a combat situation you would get rewarded with metals. I received some medals for some of the actions that I took in combat situations.

I was awarded: *The Combat Infantry Badge*
The Bronze Star
The Army Accommodation Medal with V for Valor
The Vietnam Service Medal with 2 Bronze Stars
The Purple Heart
The Army Accommodation Medal with Oak Leaf Cluster for Valor

CHAPTER 54

Going Home from Vietnam

On the way home from Vietnam our plane only made one refueling stop, it was in Manila. We were allowed to get off the plane but not to leave the airport. We were only there for about an hour and then we were back in the air and on our way to Los Angeles.

It was a long flight from Manila to Los Angeles, but we finally arrived there. We landed at the military airfield and were told that we would have to take a taxi from there to the civilian airport. Lots of taxis were lined up for us and I jumped in one side of one and another soldier jumped in from the other side. We both told the driver to take us to the civilian airport.

The other soldier was a Specialist 4th Class and he said that he was a Clerk Typist. He said, that he was glad that he didn't have to go out in the field, he had a great respect for the guys that were in the fight. He said, "I see by the metals on your uniform that you were in some bad stuff. If we have a layover when we get plane tickets home, I want to buy you a steak dinner."

On our taxi ride, we got to see the Hollywood sign on the hill, crossed the Golden Gate Bridge, and saw Alcatraz out in the bay. When we arrived at the civilian airport we both went to the desk and purchased home tickets. His was from Indianapolis, Indiana, and mine was for Tulsa, Oklahoma. He had a three-hour layover before his flight left and I had a six-hour layover before mine left. Mine was to leave at 1:00 a.m. He said let's catch a taxi and find a good steak house and I'm going to buy you that steak. We had an enjoyable dinner and afterward we walked around that part of the city until we thought that we should probably get back to the airport. We flagged down a taxi and got back to the airport in plenty of time for him to catch his flight. His flight was to leave from a different terminal than mine, so I shook his hand and thanked him for the steak dinner and told him, have a good life.

I found the terminal that I was supposed to leave from. I still had several hours before my flight was to leave. I found a USO welcome center not far from my gate. I sat and drank coffee and watched people walk by for hours. I was thinking, *Look at these free people, it looks like they have no idea what the fighting men in Vietnam are going through.*

It was almost 1:00 a.m. and I lined up to get on the plane. Five more GIs showed up and that was all that got in line. The stewardess told us to leave our bags and that they would be loaded on the plane and start down the tunnel to board the plane. We got on the plane and looked around. It was a large passenger plane with no one on it except five stewardesses that were setting in the back of the plane. One of them yelled, "Come back here, guys." So we all went to the back of the plane. One of them said, "This is all the passengers that are going to be on this flight, so you can sit anywhere you want to, but we would like for you all to sit with us." We all kind of sat in a circle. They asked us a lot of questions about Vietnam. They told jokes and stories and kept us laughing most of the time. It made the flight an enjoyable one.

Our only stop was in Beaumont, Texas. All of the GIs on the plane had to change planes. The one I got on in Beaumont was a lot different than the one that I had disembarked from as every seat was full. It was a fairly short flight from Texas to Tulsa and I arrived there about 7:00 a.m. When I was in Beaumont I had time to call my wife and tell her my estimated arrival time would be.

When I arrived in Tulsa my wife and daughter, and her uncle and aunt were there to meet me. It was a joyful meeting and a wonderful feeling just to see loved ones that I hadn't seen in a long time. My daughter didn't know me, and I would have to try to make up for the lost time with her. Again it seemed like a second life.

On the drive home when we crossed the Mayes County line it felt like home. I had a 20-day leave to enjoy the time with family and friends. On the second day back we went out to the farm to see my parents. While my dad and I were outside a high school classmate friend of mine drove up and said that he had come to buy a calf from my dad. My dad headed to the barn to get the calf ready and I opened the gate for my friend to drive through. When he drove through he asked me, "Where have you been? I haven't seen you for a while." I said that I just got back from Vietnam; that I'd been gone for a year. He said, "I didn't even know that you were in the Army." I thought no one pays any attention to anything unless it affects them.

I checked with officials at Fort Hood to see if my wife and daughter could go with me to Germany and they said, No, that there was housing only for master sergeant rank and up. After I got home someone told me to call a Chaplain and they could probably get my orders changed to stateside. I finally got a hold of a Legion Officer and he told me to go to Fort Leonard Wood, Missouri, and ask to see a Chaplain. We drove to Fort Leonard Wood and talked to a Chaplain and I told him that I had been away from my family for a year and that I didn't want to be away for six more months. He took all of my information and said let me see what I can do. He went back to his back office while we waited in the outside office. He was gone for about 20 minutes and then he came out and said, "How does Fort Hood, Texas sound?" I told him its fine with me. He said you will receive your new orders in about four days. We thanked him for his help and headed back home. We were very relieved to have my orders changed.

I received the new orders in four days and they stated that I was assigned to the 3rd Armored Division – "General Patton's Hell on Wheels," at Fort Hood, Texas. My 20-day pass was enjoyable, but it went very fast and it was time for us to go to Killeen, Texas, and Fort Hood.

CHAPTER 55
New Duty

My wife, my daughter, and I loaded our car up with all that we could and drove to Texas, two days before I was to report for duty. We knew that it would probably be hard to find a place to live because most of the soldiers coming home from Vietnam would be trying to find a place also.

We went to the Fort and asked about housing, and they said that we could stay in NCO housing for three days and then had to move out. That gave us two days to look for a place to rent. We started looking for housing in the Killeen area for the first two days without any luck everything that we found was already rented.

On the third day, I had to report for duty and when I got home that evening, we had to move out of Fort housing. Luckily, we ran into a lady from our hometown that was living there because her husband had been stationed there for some time. She said that we could stay with them until we found something to rent. We stayed with them for two days. Every evening when I got off duty we would get to search for a place to live. On the evening of the second day, we were searching about 20 miles away from the fort because one of the men in my platoon told me that there were a lot of trailer rentals in that area. We still weren't having any luck and we were afraid that I may have to move them home if we couldn't find something fairly soon. I went into a small country store and checked the bulletin board to see if any rentals were available and I asked the clerk if she knew of anything.

There was a young man at the counter, and he turned to me and said, "Are you just back from Vietnam?" I said, "Yes." He asked if I had a family and I told him that I had a wife and a baby girl. He said that he had a wife and a baby girl too. He said that he and his family stayed with someone that they didn't even know while they were trying to find some housing and that he and his wife had decided to return the favor to someone if the opportunity arose. He said, "You and your family are welcome to stay with us until something comes available for you." He said, "All we ask is that you pay for half of the food." He said that was the arrangement that they had made with the people that they stayed with. I told him it sounds good to me, let me go ask my wife. I asked her and she agreed. It was the only option that we had. So we moved in with them. Their names were Frankie and Johnny, and their baby girl was the same age as ours. What was kind of different about their names was that she was Johnny and he was Frankie. They were from Broken Arrow, Oklahoma and they were very nice people. We stayed with them for about two weeks and then we found a trailer to rent in a big trailer park on Stillhouse Hollow Lake close to Killeen, Texas.

We put what clothes and stuff that we had packed in the car in the house and then headed home for the weekend to get some more of the stuff that we needed to live there. As we were driving through the trailer park to go home all at once my car died and wouldn't start. It happened right in front of some trailers that were having a cookout party. I got out of the car and raised the hood and four guys came walking up and asked if they could help. I told them that I had just got here a few days ago and that I had been in Vietnam. The lead guy said, "You're in luck; we are all Army mechanics, we'll fix it for you." They all had a beer in their hand, and I think they were a little drunk. They went and got their toolboxes and started taking the carburetor off. They said the carburetor was probably clogged up and that they were going to take it apart and soak it in solution for a while and then put it back together. They made us go eat and drink with them while the carburetor was soaking. You couldn't ask for better treatment. When they put the carburetor back together and back on the car the mechanic that was doing it had three little parts left over in the palm of his hand. He was pretty drunk, and he looked at the parts and said, "Ah, we don't need these anyway, and he threw them in the weeds." I thought, *Oh no, we probably are not going anywhere.* He said, start her up. So I got in the car and it kicked right off. We thanked them for their hospitality and I tried to pay them but they wouldn't take anything. The lead mechanic said, "We help any GI that we can!"

We left them and headed home for the weekend and the car ran better than it ever had before. When we returned, we brought sleeping and cooking gear and we had enough necessities to make it. It was twenty miles from our trailer to the fort and I had to drive it every day. I left my wife and daughter stranded for about 12 hours every workday. When I went in, I never knew what they would have us do. Somedays we played war games, somedays we fired our weapons at moving targets and sometimes we would go on three-day bivouac. They usually wouldn't tell us beforehand so sometimes when I left it would be three days before I would be home, so it was pretty hard on her and our baby girl.

We drove home every other weekend to see family and check on our house that we kept renting even though we lived in Texas. We didn't want to lose the house. On the weekends that we didn't drive home, I would walk the bank of Stillhouse Hollow Lake and catch bass for us to eat. One time they told us the evening before that we would be going on a three-day bivouac training exercise and there was to be no alcohol allowed. As we were marching out to the site you could hear bottles clanking together in almost every GI's field jacket. When we set up camp two men were to each pup tent. Everyone broke out all the bottles of wine that they had snuck in. I never saw so much ripple wine in my life. It was really cold, so everyone took a little wine to get warm.

Sometimes when we would go home on a weekend almost everyone in our area of Texas was wearing shorts because it was hot and when we got home there may be snow on the ground. I was a platoon sergeant in the second platoon and one day for our platoon training we were to be taken out to an area that had water and inflatable rafts. We were to spend the day practicing river crossings in the boats. It was kind of fun.

About midmorning, it clouded up and the sky didn't look good. About noon a deuce and one half drove up with our lunch. They set up a tent because it looked like it was going to storm. I lined the men up. The cooks set the chow line up in a straight line about 20 yards from the tent. When the cooks were ready, I told the troops to start through the line. I always waited to be last when my men were being fed. The truck driver was in front of me in line when the last few guys were going down the chow line it started thundering and lightning and raining hard. Everyone rushed through the line and ran to get in the tent. There was one persimmon tree about halfway from the chow line to the tent. I was going through the line as fast as I could because I was getting drenched with rain. Just as I looked up to run to the tent the driver was running under the tree and lightning hit the tree. It knocked me down and I saw a big red ball of fire. Some guys in the tent ran out and dragged us into the tent. I was a little shaken up but the troop under the tree was in bad shape. There were holes blown through the bottom of his boots and he couldn't move his legs. I got on the radio and called a medical chopper. They arrived in about 15 minutes and took him away. I called the captain and informed him of what had happened and that we were still having lightning bolts hit around us. He ordered me to discontinue the training and there would be trucks to pick us up as soon as possible. I checked on the truck driver that was hit by lightning the day after and they told me that he was paralyzed from the waist down, but that there was a chance that he could recover from it over time.

I had heard from some guys that you could apply for an early out discharge if you wanted to go to college summer school. So I applied, and I got the early out. That meant that I only had eight weeks to go before I could be discharged from the Army. When I received the notice that I had been granted the early out, my wife and I decided that she and our daughter should move home. We had been paying rent on two houses and we were running out of money. I could drive home every weekend that I was off, and I could stay in the barracks with my platoon. We moved her home, also because it was hard on her being stranded and not knowing when or if I was coming home. So the next weekend we moved them and our stuff home. I drove back to the fort and moved into the barracks.

It was a ten- and half-hour drive from the fort to home. I would stay at home on the weekends for as long as I could and make it back to the fort just before time for reveille.

CHAPTER 56
Going Home for Good

My last few weeks at Fort Hood were about the same routine as when I was living off of the fort except that I ate all three meals at the fort. I assigned every member of my platoon duties in keeping the barracks clean and the tracks spotless. I rotated every man in order so that everyone had the duty when it came to their turn for it. We had an inspection one day and our latrine didn't pass. I looked on the duty list to see whose turn it was to clean it, and it was a black private. I went to his bunk and told him that he needed to go in and clean the latrine because it was his job that failed. He said, "Get off my case, man, you're picking on me!" I showed him the duty rotation list to prove that everyone had a turn at cleaning the latrine and this day had been his.

He turned to his locker and pulled a snub-nosed 38-cal revolver pistol out and pointed it at me and said, "I told you to leave me alone man!" I knew that I couldn't show any fear so I told him to put the gun back in his locker or I would take it away from him and cram it down his throat! I was very relieved when he turned around and put it back up. I went straight to the First Sergeant's Office and told him that the private had pulled a gun on me. He said, "I'll take care of it." He picked up his phone and called the MPs and they arrived shortly and handcuffed him, took his pistol, and took him away. The first sergeant told me that he would be court martialed.

One day about a week before I was to be discharged, we were sent to the motor pool for maintenance of the tracks for the whole day. We had been doing that about every other day for a while. At 5:00 p.m. the captain or a Lieutenant would show up and march us back to the barracks and then release us for the night. We would get our maintenance done and then play spades inside the tracks until it was time to march back to the company area.

At fifteen minutes after five o'clock, no one had showed up to put us in formation so I had the company fall out and into formation so that we would be ready to go when an Officer got there. Five-thirty came and still no Officer, so since I was the ranking Sergeant E-5 because I had more time in rank than any of the other platoon sergeants, I told them to get ready and that I would march the company back to the barracks. I yelled "Company" and the platoon sergeant yelled "Platoon" I gave the command right face, forward march and I called cadence all the way back. When we were about halfway back to the company area I glanced across from me and I saw the captain was marching with us. He looked at me and didn't say a thing. I thought that I might be in trouble.

The next day I received a message that I was to report to the Captain's Office, and I thought oh man… they are going to reprimand me for taking charge and marching the company back to the company area because no officer showed up to do it. I thought that I was going to get a chewing out, but instead, they congratulated me on my initiative to take charge and offered to promote me to staff sergeant E-6 if I would re-up. I politely said, "Thank you, but no thanks!"

Two weeks before my discharge date my company got orders that the whole 3rd Armored Division was going to be airlifted to Germany in a massive practice operation. The date that we were supposed to leave was just three days before my discharge date. I went to the Company Commander and asked him if I had to go to Germany because I would only have three more days left in the Army at the time that we were airlifted to Germany. He told me to stay in the Company Area and that he would see to it that I didn't have to go. I saluted him and told him, Thank you, Sir!

My early out day finally came and I put my dress uniform on to go to the processing center and do all of the paperwork to process out of the Army. After processing out in my dress uniform and feeling free, another sergeant who had processed out at the same time and I were walking down a sidewalk going to our cars and talking to each other about how glad we were to be out of the Army. We didn't notice that we had met a First Lieutenant on the sidewalk. Soon we heard, clip clop, clip clop, and heard someone running up behind us and it was the First Lieutenant. He came around in front of us and started chewing us out for not saluting him. I said, "Sir, we are no longer in this man's Army." He stepped back and saluted us and we returned the salute and he said, "Oh sorry, good luck and carry on."

I had my duffle bag already loaded in the car and headed home, hopefully for good. The feeling that I had while I was going home was like a big load had been lifted off of my shoulders. When I got home from being discharged from the Army the school had to give me my job back because I was drafted. My wife and daughter and I had very little money and it was two months before school started. I wouldn't get a paycheck until the end of the first month of school. So that meant that we would be three months without an income. I went to the employment office to file for unemployment benefits. I explained to the woman that took my case that I had been in Vietnam and that I had just gotten out of the Army and that it would be three months before I would get paid for teaching and coaching. With a very snooty attitude, she asked me, "What did the Army train you to do?" A feeling came over me that this woman has no idea of what I had been through! I told her in a stern voice, "The Army trained me to kill people! Do you have any jobs for that?" You should have seen her squirm and the blood left her face as she did a slight body shake. I thought people have no idea of what we in the infantry in Vietnam went through.

When school started, I went back to the coaching-teaching job that I had before I was Chosen to Serve. I was there for five years and then I took a principal and coaching job at a small country school that I attended as a child. I was there for fourteen years. Then I got a job at a bigger school as principal and coach. I was there for seven years. In 1998 I retired from my position as principal and coach.

I always think back to my first year as a coach and teacher and to the eighteen-year-old high school boys that I helped coach in football. Then a year later I was leading eighteen and nineteen-year-olds on search and destroy missions in the daytime and on ambushes at night in the Vietnam War. They made a sacrifice for their country and most of them were, "Chosen to Serve."

Not a day goes by that something doesn't remind me of some event that happened during my 365 days in the Republic of South Vietnam when I was "Chosen to Serve."

GLOSSARY

Fill Hole	The tern that soldiers gave for the Iron Triangle
Wolfhounds	A straight-leg infantry unit in the 27th Division
Clover Leaf	A loop-around patrol
R&R	Rest and relaxation
LCLC	Lightening Combat Leaders Course
V C	Viet Cong
NVA	North Vietnamese Army
AIT	Advanced Infantry Training
NCOIC	Non-Commissioned Officer in charge
Sit Rep	A situation report was given on the radio
Duster	M42 Combat Vehicle with twin 40MM cannons
Huey	A UH-1 Helicopter
M-72 Law	A shoulder-fired rocket launcher
PSP	Pierced steel planking with many uses
RTO	Radio telephone operator
RAG Boat	Riverine Assault Group watercraft
Mad Minute	All firing recon by fire for one minute
Dust Off	Medevac helicopter
Napalm	Jelled gasoline is mainly drooped by aircraft

Concertina Wire	Coiled barbed wire used to stop the enemy
Satchel Charge	Explosive devices used by the enemy
Track	Mechanized armored personnel carrier
Cordon	To encircle an area
Eagle Fligh	Helicopter-lifted daytime missions
Triple Duce	What the 2nd of the 22nd mechanized infantry was called
A.O.	Area of Operation
C.O.	Company Commander
The Nom	Slang term for Vietnam
Top	First Sergeant
Click	Slang for one kilometer
Cobra	AH-1 helicopter gunship
ARVN	Army Republic Vietnam
LERP	Long-range reconnaissance patrol
People Sniffer	A device that could spot living things in the dark
Sapper	An enemy with satchel charge explosives
Claymore	An electrical firing devise with 700 steel balls
Agent Orange	An herbicide used to kill vegetation
APC	Armored personnel carrier
AK47	The main enemy assault rifle
Elephant Grass	Tall grass up to 7 feet tall with sharp edges
Hooch	A Vietnamese house
Logger site	Name for the area of circled-up infantry tracks at night
WIA	Wounded in Action
KIA	Killed in Action
Point Man	The man that walked out front on patrols
Shrapnel	Metal fragments from an explosion
Star Light Scope	An optical night vision scope

Tracer	Bullets that light up to show the flight path
M-16	Standard U.S. rifle used in Vietnam
M-60	7.62 light machine gun used by U.S. troops
LZ	Landing zone for helicopters
82 MM Mortar	Used for indirect fire by U.S. troops
Bangalore Torpedoes	Seven-foot-long explosive
C-4 Explosives	Plastic explosives with many uses
Det Chord	A thin tube filled with C-4 is used to chain explosives together

Printed in the USA
CPSIA information can be obtained
at www.ICGtesting.com
LVHW042058160124
768961LV00006B/243